JACK GIBSON, FRCSI, DTM&H (Lond.), graduated from the Royal College of Surgeons, Dublin, in 1933, having won almost every available medal. He gained the Fellowship in 1934 (the youngest ever to be awarded this distinction, at the age of 25) and the Diploma of Tropical Medicine and Hygiene from London in 1935. He then took two locums, one in Aden and the second in Malawi. After a hospital appointment in England, he returned to Africa as Dean of the Native Medical Arts School, forerunner of the present Durban Medical School. After the outbreak of war, he worked in England as a surgeon in the hospitals of the Emergency Medical Service. Back in Ireland, he took up the post of County Surgeon in Naas, Co. Kildare, and continued to develop his method of deep relaxation as an alternative to anaesthetics and drugs, performing over 4,000 operations using hypnosis alone. Since his retirement from surgery in 1979, he has devoted his time to the treatment of psychosomatic disorders using hypnotherapy. He is a member of the Irish and British Societies of Clinical and Experimental Hypnosis, and the International Society of Hypnosis.

D0743795

WHAT THEY'RE SAYING ABOUT THIS BOOK:

Dr P.J. Browne, FRCPsych., DPM, President of the Irish Society of Clinical and Experimental Hypnosis:
'This is a most entertaining book which I can warmly recommend, not only to medical colleagues but to the general public. It is a fascinating account of the use of hypnosis by Surgeon Jack Gibson in his treatment of various psychosomatic illnesses and of his extensive use of hypnosis over a period of thirty years as an aid to early intervention in the treatment of acute surgical trauma. This "man for all seasons" has most interesting philosophical views on education and on the treatment of smoking and alcoholism.'

Dr Godfrey J.F. Briggs, MBBS, DPM, RNR, Former President of the British Society of Medical and Dental Hypnosis:
'I have known Jack Gibson as a very dedicated surgeon since before the Second World War. His active and enquiring mind, and his compassion for people, has led him to recognise the value of hypnosis in the alleviation of all forms of suffering. Since his retirement as a surgeon, he has widened his field considerably and extended his therapy into medicine as a whole. As a result of his experiences, he has written this intriguing book. Primarily it is a book for laymen, but the increasing number of professional men who are becoming dissatisfied with the pharmacological and electronic exuberance of our age will find much to encourage and sustain their desire to become better doctors.'

Pan Collins, Senior Researcher for over two decades for *The Late Late Show*, Ireland's top-rating TV show for the past 27 years:
'On 13 October 1969, I listened to Jack Gibson's record *How to stop Smoking* for the first and only time in my life. As a contented chain-smoker of 37 years, I had no desire to give up my coffin nails and to this day my warcry is, "I didn't give up cigarettes — they gave me up." That was 20 years ago and I have never smoked another cigarette.
It is high time Jack Gibson wrote of his experience as a medical hypnotist. The life of the man who has performed surgery on people under hypnosis, even to amputations, where a patient's condition would not tolerate an anaesthetic, is striking testimony to the efficacy of hypnotherapy when undertaken by a medically qualified practitioner. When the book's author is also a good storyteller, it makes for a very good read.'

Life and Times of An Irish Hypnotherapist

DR JACK GIBSON
FRCSI, DTM&H (Lond.)

THE MERCIER PRESS
CORK & DUBLIN

The Mercier Press Limited
4 Bridge Street, Cork, &
24 Lower Abbey Street, Dublin 1

Copyright © Jack Gibson, 1989

All rights reserved. No part of this publication may be
reproduced, stored in a retrieval system, or transmitted
in any form or by any means, electronic, photocopying,
recording or otherwise, without the prior permission in
writing from the publisher.

British Library Cataloguing in Publication Data
Gibson, Jack
    Life and times of an Irish hypnotherapist.
    1. Medicine. Hypnotherapy – Biographies
    I. Title
    615.8'512'0924

ISBN 0 85342 911 1

*The names of the patients in this book have been
changed to protect their privacy and identity.*

Typeset in Palatino by Seton Music Graphics,
Bantry, Co Cork
Printed and bound in Ireland by Leinster Leader Ltd.,
Naas, Co Kildare

Contents

Dedicated to

THE IRISH SOCIETY OF
CLINICAL AND EXPERIMENTAL HYPNOSIS

A group of dedicated people who
look on the welfare of everybody
as their greatest aim

Foreword
by
Dr R. C. Coombes, PhD, MD, MRCP
Consultant, St George's Hospital, London

It gives me great pleasure to write this foreword. The last two decades have witnessed a revolution in health and this is largely due to the increased demand of ordinary individuals to understand more fully the causes of disease. Unfortunately, the medical profession has not been able to fulfil this need until fairly recently. Jack Gibson was one of the pathfinders in the field of alternative medicine. At a time when dietary theories of disease, hypnosis, acupuncture and other alternative therapeutic methods were regarded as worthless, he was already pioneering a radical new approach to the treatment of common diseases. Publications, recordings and lectures, detailing his wide, perhaps unequalled, experience with hypnosis have helped many individuals in their battle against disease and in their fight to overcome ignorance of the mechanisms of common ailments.

One of the unique features of Jack Gibson's work has been his insistence that the only real way of overcoming disease ('dis-ease') is by putting the patient at his or her ease. Of course, this can be initiated with the help of a trained person, but subsequently the concept of relaxation and 'being at ease' with oneself is something that has to be done frequently and regularly by the person himself. Jack has realised this and most of his work has been in evolving methods of self-instruction.

The concept that self-cure exists is, of course, contrary to a good deal of conventional medical thought. But more and more people are now becoming aware that the combination of diet, relaxation, exercise and awareness can prevent, ameliorate or even cure most of the ailments common in our society.

In this book the author has focused on a relatively small number of ailments. The reader should not be deceived into thinking that these are the only problems that can be helped by relaxation. I have been working in the field of cancer for many years past and even in this difficult area patients can be helped significantly by relaxation techniques, particularly to obtain

7

control of pain and other unpleasant symptoms associated with cancer. As to the all-important question of the causes of cancer, there are now increasing numbers of epidemiologists who believe that diet is one of the principal causes of cancer in our society. Individuals who have been born in a non-Westernised part of the world develop high instances of cancer of the breast, colon and lung, which are the major killer-cancers in our society, only when they move to Western Europe or North America and adopt those countries' eating habits. Those individuals who maintain the dietary habits of their parent country rarely develop Western forms of cancer.

Clearly, stress and smoking have much to do with various disease processes. Jack Gibson suggests several effective measures for controlling the stress that can lead to bad dietary habits and heavy smoking. There is no doubt in my mind that adoption of these simple techniques, in combination with more sensible eating and drinking, would contribute to a marked decline in disease in our society over the next generation.

As we can see in this admirable book, the way to a healthier society is not through the development of new and better drugs, to sedate and palliate large numbers of people. I am absolutely convinced that a healthier society will result only from an awareness on the part of each individual of the power of his or her own mind. The medical profession needs more members of Jack Gibson's calibre in order to be certain that his message is driven home.

R. C. C.
June 1989, London

INTRODUCTION
The Subconscious Mind

It was before I took up hypnotherapy. An old lady, I'll call her Mrs O__, had cancer and lay dying in hospital. Unfortunately, an advanced secondary condition had been discovered, 'roots' — in lay terminology, a cancerous growth that had spread beyond the point where it is possible for the surgeon to cure. I had been increasing the amounts of opium and other pain-killing drugs given to her each day. Every drug at our disposal had been tried and I had increased the dose, as I always did, to the stage where it might prove fatal, but nothing had the power to alleviate the pain for long. Eventually we reached the stage where no drug was effective at all.

The poor woman was in unbearable agony and those of us who attended her felt dreadful. One day we took her to the operating theatre and removed a piece of bone from her skull; I put a knife through the subconscious part of the brain. (This operation, then coming into vogue, is known as a leucotomy. But some operations come in and out of vogue at the speed of high fashion and it was replaced soon afterwards by the discovery of new drugs which, for a time, were described as causing a 'medical leucotomy'.) The next day I went into the ward and asked Mrs O__ how she felt. To my disappointment she replied, 'Just the same', but immediately volunteered some news she had been reading in the morning paper and asked me what I thought about it. She was completely unconcerned about her pain. In a few days she was up and dressed. Later, she was discharged from hospital and died at home, among her own people.

The subconscious mind is something we can explore and harness to our advantage or ignore at our peril. It is a source of enormous potential energy. It is the computer with all the information. It is the harbinger of all our hidden fears. It is the guardian of our sleep. It regulates the quantities of hormones produced by our ductless glands. It can be held responsible for our actions as extroverts or introverts. It can make us afraid of heights or spiders or open spaces, or fearless in the face of danger.

If we do not understand our subconscious mind, then we cannot understand why the hazel rod turns down in the water-diviner's hand or why the wheeze occurs in the asthmatic. We cannot understand ourselves. But if we do, many of life's problems are solved. The pieces of the jigsaw fit into place. The asthmatic can breathe without wheezing, the stammerer can speak normally, phobias can be dealt with — in fact, all of us who are suffering from psychosomatic disorders can find a new lease of life.

Most probably, as you read this, every single minute some person will die from smoking, some child will be beaten by an alcoholic parent and other people will die from psychosomatic disorders. All senseless and useless suffering. All of it preventable.

The subconscious mind is an unusual piece of mechanism. It will be seen from the cases I have treated that a great number come within the limit of what is usually looked on as only 20 per cent. But there is a reason for this. Those who come into hospital having been involved in, for example, a car accident are brought in totally defenceless at the mercy of any of us, but with the hope that something can be done to alleviate their suffering. In other words, the 'spunk' has been knocked out of them. The man who is resistant to hypnosis and who would answer in the ordinary way if asked 'which will you have, a general anaesthetic or hypnosis?' would almost invariably opt for a general anaesthetic. But when he comes into hospital bleeding, in pain and having had a full meal some hours beforehand, he is not a suitable case for a general anaesthetic. He will accept without question that his wounds must be stitched and the bleeding stopped, or his fracture set without delay. When he is told that if he relaxes he will feel less pain, and if he relaxes deeply enough he won't even feel the local anaesthetic, then when it is seen that no pain is felt by the needle being inserted, no anaesthetic is given. It will be useful for other doctors to look out for the percentage of people to whom this may apply, for I did not know the importance of these statistics when I was working in the hospital.

For over 30 years, I have practised the healing art of hypno-therapy, to control the subconscious mind and so eliminate pain during and after trauma. As a surgeon, I have performed some 4,000 operations using its techniques. I know it works and so do thousands of patients.

PART I: THE METHOD

1: First Encounters

It could have been in any city in Africa or the East, where such practices are common. It happened to be in Durban, where as a young doctor, in 1958, I had taken up a post as surgical partner in a medical practice. It was there that I began to grasp the opportunity of studying the various methods being used to reach the subconscious mind and to appreciate the many ways in which mind control can be used effectively in everyday medicine.

I had been in general practice before, in England. As a student in Dublin's Royal College of Surgeons, I had been well taught about the physical side of medicine. But I had received almost no training in the causes or treatment of most of the illnesses I was to meet. I had been taught to treat asthmatics with cortisone and bronchial dilators; I had seen the attacks disappear for a time, but always they returned. I had treated bed-wetters by making them sleep less heavily, but this method gave only slight relief — the cause remained untouched. I had given pain-killers and hormones to sufferers from migraine, but their attacks persisted. I had given rheumatoid-arthritis victims cortisone and aspirin, which gave them temporary relief. I saw the addicts of drugs, alcohol and nicotine listen to my advice, only to reject it. I saw most of my overweight patients continue to bulge — unless they used that most damnable of drugs, dexetrin. (I use the word 'damnable' because dexetrin tended to be used in such quantities as to destroy the patterns of sleep and open the pathway to other drugs. In Ireland, incidentally, the drug is now banned.) I treated insomniacs with sedatives; some became better, but none were cured of the underlying cause of their inability to sleep.

All this time I had been continually reading and searching in the hope of finding something better, of more lasting value to my patients. I was beginning to realise how so much of human misery had its origin in the mind. I began to develop an unquenchable desire to tap the subconscious, which I recognised as a great source of potential energy. I felt inadequate in that I had often seen others reach the subconscious mind effectively and frequently. I did not, however, always like what I had seen. What

I disliked is akin to what has turned Seventh Day Adventists, Jehovah's Witnesses and countless others, believer and sceptic, away from hypnosis. Up to this time, I had seen hypnosis used mainly for entertainment; this always seemed to contain some element of danger, especially in the use of post-hypnotic suggestions made for 'fun' and to demonstrate the involuntary control of one person by another.

This book is, in the main, an account of how over the years of my professional life I have used a method of hypnosis that is the complete opposite of this 'show business' approach. What I found, and wished to teach others, was a technique for gaining control over *ourselves* and freeing the mind, and thereby the body, from influences which are harmful. If, at any time, someone wanted to hypnotise us against our will after we have learned mind control, it would be difficult to the point of impossibility. Self-hypnosis is the art of creating harmony in the mind, of helping the subconscious and the conscious to work together for our own good. Consequently, there is nothing in mind control that is inconsistent with anything from the Hippocratic Oath to conservative theology.

In the decades that have passed since I first began to study this subject, other forms of conditioning the subconscious have become increasingly popular. Torrents of words have been written and spoken about this or that alternative medicine; neophilosophical and quasi-religious organisations have sprung up, concerned with the pursuit of health, happiness and 'enlightenment'. If we *are* going to be happy, we need to understand ourselves more fully and not act like the lemmings who follow each other to their own destruction or like those whose minds and bodies have been manipulated to such an extent that they feel they cannot live without drugs, cigarettes, alcohol, over-eating, over-spending and the rest of the century's salient malaises. If one is inclined to say, 'I'll let no one interfere with my subconscious mind' while still unable to free oneself from one of these addictions, let there be no mistake — the subconscious mind has already been reached. Until harmony is restored, there can be no progress towards a more perfect peace and health.

I had hardly started work in the Durban partnership when I received a challenge. I was called to see a man who was ill and confined to bed. I found his sheets spotted with burn holes from the cigarettes he smoked while dropping off to sleep. The presence of his three children in the house increased my concern and I felt the need to do everything in my power to stop the worst from happening. I treated the man for his illness with 'orthodox' medicine and returned later to see if I could do something about his smoking habit. This was my first attempt at hypnosis and I was elated when the man went into a deep trance; to test the efficacy of my method, I gave him a post-hypnotic suggestion which he immediately carried out. As a result I was no longer worried about the house catching fire: I had broken the man from smoking, or so I believed, and felt considerable satisfaction at having done so. But I remained aware that I had not removed from his subconscious the things that made him smoke. I did, however, regard myself as an initiate in the art of hypnosis from that time and subsequently abandoned many of the methods I had been using. From then on I tried self-hypnosis on any case that seemed to warrant it.

Soon afterwards, I received a call from a woman whose leg had become paralysed. Naturally, I was hoping that the condition would prove to be psychosomatic and, when she told me that she was pregnant for the third time after only three years of marriage, I felt that this was the most likely explanation. When she added that she had become temporarily blind on one occasion, then the diagnosis became almost certain. She also revealed the fact that her husband was utterly unconcerned about her having been pregnant for almost their entire married life.

Now if this woman's paralysis were a protective mechanism, then hypnotic suggestion by itself (such as I had used with the man who might have set his house ablaze) would have been dangerous. The patient had first of all to come to grips with her problems and only when she felt that she could manage her present pregnancy, and speak frankly with her husband about the distress she was feeling, did I hypnotise her. When she entered into a trance, she moved her formerly paralysed leg normally. Having learnt how to face her situation with equanimity, her leg would probably have moved normally in time anyway, but she now had the satisfaction of walking around her house, cured after one session. It was not the return of the use of her limb, however, which intrigued me as much as what followed.

The woman asked me to attend her at home for the birth of her baby. The question was, could hypnosis be used for a completely normal birth, controlling the muscles and alleviating or eliminating all pain. In due course I was called. It was four o'clock in the afternoon and the woman had been awake the whole of the previous night with labour pains. I was disappointed at not having been called sooner. The midwife who was looking after her was working according to rule and knew nothing about painless childbirth. I began counting and within half a minute, the mother-to-be was in a deep trance. She cooperated totally during the labour and the baby was born with ease, without a tear shed. Only when the afterbirth was passed did I ask her to wake up. During the 25 minutes that had passed since I had entered her house (and it *was* actually only 25), she had responded so completely that she now felt fresh and alert. The next day, she told me that she had had her friends in after the birth and had been able to entertain them until ten o'clock that night without any trace of fatigue. Since this was despite her having been awake the whole of the previous night, I felt that here was something that could be of benefit to all women.

It was due to this experience and similar cases that followed that I was led to make the record (and later the cassette) *Painless Childbirth*, which gives women the choices ranging from painless participation to complete oblivion. This is an area in which the variations in experience are countless, but I have been encouraged through the years by the numbers of women who have reported back to me their satisfaction with the techniques contained on the record. The simple basis of these techniques, and the principle that underlies what in recent years has come to be called 'mother-centered' childbirth, is that if we are tense, pain is intensified and if we relax, pain is relieved. If we relax totally, pain is abolished.

Asthma, particularly among children, is an universal complaint from which thousands die each year. It would be difficult to count the number of those who progress to bronchial asthma, often dying from worn-out hearts which for years have been straining to pump blood through constricted lungs. When I had worked in general practice previously, one of the most distressing cases I had to deal with was that of a little boy who would beat his head against the wall during his asthmatic attacks. All I had been able to prescribe were pills, an inhaler and injections. The attacks continued and so did the almost unbearable sight of this wretched child inflicting pain upon himself.

After my first experiments with hypnotherapy, however, I felt that I now had one more weapon in my armamentarium and it was not long before I had an opportunity to use it. One day an Indian doctor brought her niece to see me in my Durban surgery. The girl suffered so severely with asthma, and the attacks were so frequent, that it was thought she was subnormal. For years, ever since she had been involved in a swimming accident in which her friend had drowned, she had been wheezing as though the muscles in her bronchial tubes were trying to prevent her from inhaling water. Her aunt told me she was morose, sat by herself, took no part in anything and was very backward. After treatment with hypnosis, the wheezing diminished, the girl was happier, she stopped missing time from school and, at her next examination three months later, to our great joy, she had moved from the bottom of a class of 45 to the top.

I was very aware at this stage that I had an enormous amount still to learn about the use of hypnotherapy. I was a neophyte in the field. But in this case, the origin of the child's illness — in the trauma of the drowning incident — was so apparent that its significance could scarcely be lost on me. I pondered on the implications.

2: Mind Control

I was working in Durban when I first started my study of hypnotherapy — long before acupuncture, transcendental meditation, yoga and other forms of Eastern practice became common in the West. I was fascinated by the many ways in which the subconscious mind was being reached all around me at the time.

'Fire-walking' was perhaps the most dramatic of these demonstrations in the control of the mind. The fire-walkers were Indians who had originally been brought to Natal to work on the sugar plantations; they had brought their Hindu culture and religion with them. Each year during one of the great religious festivals, an enormous fire would be lit and the red-hot coals spread out on the ground. Those who were going to walk over the embers spent three days in preparation, which included the continual beating of drums, by the end of which time they were in a trance. Then they walked over the fire without the sensation or appearance of burning. The reason why remains a medical mystery. The Indians believe that it is the spirits of their ancestors who enter into them and so allow them to walk unharmed over the burning embers. (To make sure that the fire was really hot, I removed my own shoes, took one quick step and raised a blister on my foot.)

However, the places where I found the greatest enlightenment in regard to hypnotic techniques were those which I approached and studied with an ambiguity of attitude which to this day I have not entirely resolved. The use of hypnosis for the purpose of public entertainment has been banned by the medical profession in many countries, since it is felt that the human mind should not be manipulated for mere amusement. This is the reason why I feel so strongly that for therapeutic purposes, *self-hypnosis* is to be the first and most important objective — the method, in other words, whereby we ourselves find our own release from the influences which have upset the normal workings of our minds.

Hypnosis for public entertainment was not outlawed in Durban and I must admit to having learned an enormous amount from these shows. It has to be said that these public entertainments can be hilarious and the dangers are incomparably less than in, say, boxing where the primary aim is to knock out the opponent, which concusses his brain and can have the serious after-effect of making him 'punch-drunk'. After hypnosis entertainments, I have never seen damage to the brain, although I have known people engage in dangerous activities. I once saw a young man chasing a bus, oblivious to every thought but that of catching the leprechaun which he believed to be his and which he had seen in a visual hallucination inside the bus. This young man, who later became my patient when I returned to Ireland, had been subjected several times to stage hypnosis; I will give a more detailed account of his case on p. 99. It is largely because of such post-hypnotic suggestions that many medical practitioners have been so adamantly opposed to the use of hypnosis as a form of public entertainment. But there is so much that can be learned from stage hypnosis that we must keep our minds open and sometimes let our reservations lapse in the interests of a wider knowledge.

Superficially, it seems medical men come a poor second when their methods of hypnosis are compared to the gaudier techniques of the stage entertainers. The fact is, however, that the stage performers have their own methods of selection and the audience is usually totally unaware of how carefully they work in order to carry these out. First of all, the hypnotist may ask each member of the audience to place his or her hands together, fingers entwined, palms upward over their heads — excusing those who do not wish to be involved and thus, probably, would not make good subjects, thereby making the first step in the selection process. Those who have their hands over their heads are then told that some of them will find it impossible to pull their hands apart. In actual fact, it is physically difficult to do this anyway with the palms upward; if one is even slightly suggestible, it is impossible. At this juncture, those who are liable not to be good subjects will turn their hands to one side or, with slight difficulty, disengage their fingers. Those who fail to separate their hands are now a selected group and are asked to come up on stage. A few will disengage their fingers on the way, but those who do arrive are now in the limelight, looking forward to an evening's entertainment. It is at this point that the major difference between the subject on the stage and the patient on the operating table is apparent.

The desire to look well in the sight of others is an inherent part of our nature. But we cannot all be entertainers, so we cooperate with the stage hypnotist. Each person now on stage knows that he or she is part of a show which will make people rollick with laughter. Each 'volunteer' is happy to cooperate with the hypnotist. They know that they may be asked to perform absurd acts, but it is all part of the fun and others will be doing the same. They are on stage. They are entertaining.

The man on the operating table, in contrast, is not there out of choice; he may be there following a car crash — not selected out of a willingness to create merriment. He fears that he will feel pain. He may think that hypnosis is all very fine but — a general anaesthetic would be more reliable. Similarly, a person undergoing treatment to stop smoking, or for asthma, has not been selected. If we in the medical profession can achieve an almost 100 per cent success rate in these areas, then it is the stage hypnotist who would appear to be the poor second, leaving aside any ethical considerations of the comparative motives of the two.

We must, however, in fairness say that even in medical conditions, there is sometimes a form of selection. Those who suffer from complaints such as asthma or certain types of skin disease have their illnesses because their subconscious has had a tendency to react to something unpleasant. Since the subconscious has reacted already, it is usually easy to get it to react again — positively.

To return to the stage hypnotist and those who cannot separate their hands without help — these people will be hypnotised more and more deeply, and they will love it. They can hear the audience laughing at them, but they don't mind — they are enjoying themselves. Those who are slightly dubious about what they are doing will come out of the trance. The hypnotist, if he has enough people on stage, will send them back to their seats; if he hasn't, he will endeavour to put them back into a trance and to deepen it even further. As they perform one act after another, their trance becomes deeper.

There is a counterpart to this process in surgery: as with the stage performance, where each act leads to a deeper state of trance, so with surgery if it is necessary to operate under hypnosis for any length of time, it is easy to implant post-hypnotic suggestions which can keep the patient free from discomfort over the entire stay in hospital.

The stage performer is usually considered by the audience to have a 'gift' and this idea is naturally encouraged by the production of dramatic effects. The medical hypnotist, conversely, has the responsibility of trying to let the patient know that he has no gift, that it is the patient's *own* attitude of mind that is essential for the success of the treatment. Comparisons may be odious, but they are sometimes important: this one will end with the final, reiterated statement that stage hypnosis and self-hypnosis are, quite essentially, direct opposites of each other.

Why do these unrehearsed hypnosis shows produce as much laughter as any contrived comedy? I think it is because the most ordinary people are capable of doing the most extraordinary, unexpected and comical things. Their abandonment of all reticence, accompanied by a readiness to sing and mime and, in fact, do anything to create laughter is capitalised on. The look of astonishment on the faces of the hypnotised subjects creates great amusement in itself. Anticipation is at its height, since no one knows what is going to happen next, but whatever it is, one can be sure it will be dramatic. And hovering over it all is the sense of danger, with subjects falling to the floor or leaping around the stage on the command words of the hypnotist. But no one ever seems to get hurt.

One really needs to see the unrestrained actions of people on a stage and the expressions on their faces to realise the depth of their release from self-consciousness. The words 'sleep' and 'relax' may be used as a signal for people to go into a deeper hypnotic trance. A man may walk nonchalantly onto the stage after his hands have been released, fall to the floor in a trance at the command of the hypnotist and lie there immobile until roused. Others on stage may be told they are going on a picnic and they will walk along as if doing so, until they are told to sit down. They may then be told that there are ants running about and they will leap to their feet, pulling off shoes and socks to scratch the imaginary insects. 'Now they are running all over your body,' the hypnotist may say and the people start to tear at their clothes, scratching madly; it may only be when they seem prepared to strip off entirely that the situation will be stopped. The utterly natural expressions of wild agitation and frantic scratching have no parallel with rehearsed acting. They will then be told that the ants are gone and that they can wake up. With genuine expressions of relief, the 'performers' will put their shoes back on and replace any clothing they may have removed.

This 'itching' act is easily induced or obliterated. In fact, hypnotic suggestion is used medically with those who suffer from skin irritations. When the irritation caused by the rash is removed by suggestion, the improvement in the rash itself is usually dramatic.

Back on stage, a man may be asked the name of his favourite actress and then told that she is here and wants to dance with him. He will be handed a mop, which he will take and ogle and cuddle and dance with in sheer delight, oblivious to the screams of laughter coming from the audience. If a man appears to be a person of some dignity, he may be told that when he wakens he will go back to his seat, but that when he sits down he will receive an electric shock. All the hypnotist has to do if he wants the man back on stage is to tell him to come back. The man walks down the aisle. People watch in anticipation. They see him sit down and then spring up from the seat, not knowing what on earth has happened. He might look for somewhere else.to sit, but each time he receives an electric shock. This will carry on until the hypnotist has milked the situation dry and decides to have mercy and move on to another act. On other occasions, the hypnotist may place a burning match under someone's hand or push needles into them, without causing any pain. The audience watches spellbound.

I have seen shows where, on one side of the stage, a man was milking an imaginary cow (the fingers of a glove, in fact) with great enthusiasm, while all over the stage people were doing equally bizarre things with a realism and application that kept the audience enthralled. One routine from those pre-permissive days involved the subjects being told that they were in Paris, in front-row seats at the Moulin Rouge, and that nude girls of indescribable beauty would appear before them. The unrestrained lubricity of the men and the utter boredom of the women sent the audience into paroxysms of mirth.

At some point regression may be demonstrated, with people being brought back in time to their early childhood. Grown men, regressed to infancy, will cry for their mothers with a realism that could never be reproduced, even by the most talented of actors. Perhaps the subjects will be told that they are sitting at their schooldesks. A middle-aged man will be called out by the 'teacher' and told to write 'cat' on the blackboard, which he might do in unsteady, block capital letters, possibly putting them in the wrong order as he used to do at an early age. He may be brought forward a couple of years and his writing will have improved and his spelling will be better. While he is doing this, someone else in the 'class' may pinch the person in front or pull their hair; another may put up their hand and ask to be excused.

At the end of the show, the audience will have seen a great deal of hidden talent, feats of strength performed by average people, the inducement of hallucinations and anaesthesia (lack of physical feeling), the regression of time — all things of immense use in medicine for diagnosis and treatment. Even sceptical members of the audience and those who may be troubled by the ethics of what they have seen will leave such an entertainment somewhat baffled, perhaps with a modicum of apprehension, and certainly with their minds seething with questions. The salient one for a medical person will be how these faculties of mind can be used for good in the treatment of disease? This question is the central theme of this book.

The plate on the door read 'Hypnotist'. I went in, introduced myself and was most cordially received. We had a long talk and I learned that the hypnotist had been at this work for many years, achieving particularly good results in the treatment of asthma. He told me how he had found bed-wetting much more difficult to treat. I was, at that time, unable to help him; it was not until many years later that I found it to be one of the easiest conditions to cure, an explanation and practice in self-hypnosis with a cassette being all that was necessary. He then went on to describe a case on which he was working with great enthusiasm. I felt sorry for him because I knew he was heading for failure. The case concerned a man who had had a nerve resected, or partially cut out, from his arm. The hypnotist believed that there were fifteen other nerves capable of doing the same work, but as a doctor I knew there were no such nerves.

My next encounter with 'hypnotherapy' was with a speech therapist. Although she knew nothing about hypnosis and had never heard of its use for speech therapy, she felt there was something in her method of treatment which made it work beyond her expectations. In her rooms, she showed me her methods and played several recordings of people's voices before, during and after treatment. (As cassettes and tape-recorders had not yet come into general use, these recordings had been laboriously cut as gramophone discs.) We listened to a record of a person stammering very badly. She told him to relax and listen to her counting; when she had counted to 30, she asked him to speak again. This time there was a marked improvement. At the end of the session she told him that she had finished treatment for that day, but was going to count backwards from 30 to 1 before he would get up from the couch. This therapist was actually doing all her work using hypnosis, yet she had no idea that this was, in part, the basis for her good results.

I witnessed another example of someone who was using hypnosis unknown to themselves. At the end of the ballet class, the teacher wanted her pupils to have a short rest, so she asked them to lie on the floor and then said, 'Think of the sea going out, and the sea coming in, the sea going out, the sea coming in ...' She continued this chant slowly and quietly until the children closed their eyes and rested, breathing evenly and deeply.

Dr Dormer was a close friend of mine and the head of a large tuberculosis hospital in Durban. He was among the most orthodox medical men I have ever known. He had one group of children who were beyond any form of treatment known to him, except that given by an 80-year-old woman with no medical background whom he employed. He told me that he did not know how she gained her results. The children were being treated for tuberculosis meningitis when streptomycin had first been discovered. They were totally blind and deaf, and unable to use their limbs, yet she was getting through to them. I set out to find the basis of this treatment and discovered that the woman's belief was that vibrations were being transmitted through the atmosphere to her, which she, in turn, passed on to the children. Her own hands seemed to vibrate as she held them. She was obviously creating a 'rapport', reaching the deepest part of their minds and thus gaining a response. I later found out she practised yoga.

After that incident, I was invited to attend a gathering of yoga practitioners. Three thousand people turned up, mostly Indians but including a wide range of other nationalities. It was a beautiful day and everyone seemed happy to be there. One person was handing out little bags of food and the whole atmosphere generated was one of serenity and contentment. The multitude stood in the open, while addresses were made by people of every colour and race. We heard about people whose lives were tranquil and whose ages far exceeded the normal life-span. An attempt was made to send vibrations to some miners who were trapped underground near Johannesburg, with the intoning of one word, which to my ears would have been spelled 'o-h-m'. This word occurred frequently since it was believed to be connected with special power. One person with a pleasant voice sang each phrase beginning with 'ohm' and, concentrating on the body from the spine in the neck downward, we were told to think of any parts of our bodies in which we had pain. There was no doubt in my mind that this pleasant hypnotic repetition would, with susceptible people, quickly reach the subconscious mind and that the pain would disappear. These good people, it transpired, were hoping to build a hospital. I felt that if they tried the techniques of yoga for the treatment of organic illnesses, they would be bound to meet with failure. But if they applied their techniques to treating psychosomatic complaints, they might well be successful.

The professor of psychology at the Durban Medical School

once described to me a piece of research work that had come to his attention. A man he knew had small cancerous growths on the back of both his hands (known as epitheliomas); these are quite common and not particularly dangerous unless neglected over a long period. The professor's colleague had hypnotised the man and told him that one of the growths would disappear. The other was left untreated. Some time later, both growths were removed and sent to a pathologist for examination. The pathologist had not been told about the hypnosis treatment. When the report came back, the untreated growth was indicated as 'an epithelioma', with no further comments; the treated one was described as 'epithelioma, apparently treated with radiation'.

One of my first operations using hypnotherapy was performed in the McCord Zulu Hospital, where I worked just before the Second World War. Miss S____ was a charming young lady in her late teens; her face, however, was painfully disfigured by lumps, blackheads, minute scars and pustules. I trained her in self-hypnosis, so that she was able to produce the correct hormones from the various glands that control the condition of the skin. She was also trained to take away all feeling from her face so that an operation could be carried out with ease. This involved, firstly, removing pieces of skin from over the small abscesses and then a 'sandpapering' treatment to remove the surface skin from the entire face.

A number of doctors in the hospital wished to see hypnotherapy in action. Despite the stringent colour bar and no matter how hard people tried to dissuade her, Miss S____ volunteered to be the subject of the demonstration. The idea of showing how those distressing septic spots on her face could be cured painlessly far outweighed all others. She got up on the operating table in the presence of a theatre-full of doctors (African, Indian and European), lay down and within perhaps fifteen seconds was in a deep trance. Using ordinary sandpaper, I began to rub her face vigorously, since the scar tissue was extremely tough; it bled quite profusely, but this was easily controlled in the usual way with pads pressed on the parts already 'sanded', while I worked on the next area. One of the Indian doctors, who saw the advantages of being able to operate without an anaesthetist, asked me if Miss S____ had to forgo her breakfast, as would a patient who was going to have a general anaesthetic. I told him to ask her directly, so while her face was being forcefully scrubbed, she explained calmly to him how she had taken her breakfast as usual that morning. When the operation was over, she sat up and had her face dressed. She declined a lift home, saying that she felt perfectly well, would prefer to walk the mile or so home and did not in the least mind anyone seeing her swathed in bandages.

Another experience taught me how hypnotherapy could be used to counter false beliefs. A Zulu woman came to see me, complaining that she vomited every Wednesday without fail. New sects were continually springing up in Africa and the preacher of the one to which this woman belonged had told his congregation that they would vomit on a certain day in each week. The successful implantation of such an idea would be child's play for anyone adept at hypnotic technique and working with ideally receptive minds. Having put the woman into a trance, I simply told her that the condition was in her mind, that there was nothing physically wrong with her and that next Wednesday would be the same as any other day. Naturally, she stopped vomiting.

Throughout this book, there are many stories sufficient to prove that we are being manipulated in more ways than we realise.

3: Hypnosis in Surgery

For twenty years, up until my retirement as a surgeon in 1979, I worked to try and introduce hypnosis into surgical wards as an accepted form of treatment. I believe hypnosis to be as effective as antibiotics; of course, antibiotics will cure diseases which hypnosis cannot help, but hypnosis can cure cases where antibiotics are of no use whatsoever.

The work of introducing hypnosis as a routine treatment was quietly and unobtrusively going forward when, one day, a reporter was sent from an English newspaper to investigate my recording *How to stop smoking,* which uses, among other things, hypnotic techniques. He had been dispatched because his editor had read accounts of people who had quit smoking with the aid of this record and who had experienced no desire to smoke again. It so happened that the day the reporter arrived, I was performing an amputation on a severe cardiac case. The patient had a gangrenous leg, a failing heart and diabetes. The anaesthetist was not happy about giving him an anaesthetic, so I decided to take the leg off using a combination of local anaesthetic and hypnosis. The patient turned out to be a good subject for hypnosis, as so many are when their case is desperate. When he came into the operating theatre, he was happy and full of fun despite his failing heart. He enjoyed the hypnosis and, in fact, said afterwards that for the first time he felt free from pain and when his leg was being sawn off he actually enjoyed the procedure! On his return from the operation, he asked for some 'crubeens', an old Irish dish made from pigs' trotters. In fact, he did not miss a single meal; his diabetes was unaffected and his overall well-being maintained.

The English reporter, seeing the possibility of a scoop, wanted the story and a photograph of the patient. I told him he would have to sign a letter stating that he would not mention my name or that of the hospital. He agreed, the story subsequently appeared and anonymity was kept. But in a few days, other newspapers had discovered my name and where I worked — I had a lot of explaining to do to the General Medical Council!

Hypnosis is best carried out by an anaesthetist and a surgeon, both of whom know its value and how to use it. But anyone trained in the uses of hypnosis can keep a patient in a relaxed state. It is hoped that more and more anaesthetists will adopt the method. I was using it in the early days, when only very occasionally had I someone to keep the patient hypnotised.

Hypnosis has proved invaluable in accident work particularly, since most patients arrive without their stomachs being empty, which precludes a general anaesthetic. Moreover, the length of time it takes for a stomach to empty following an accident can be much longer than when a person is in normal health. Under hypnosis, it is possible to operate without delay.

It has always been my hope that eventually hypnosis will assume a much larger role in the workings of hospitals of the future. In Australia, for example, hypnosis is now taught to medical students in most universities and they have the opportunity of seeing it used and using it themselves in their hospitals — as seen in a recent episode of the popular medical 'soap', *The Flying Doctors*.

SOME CASE HISTORIES

Mr J____ was a professional footballer. One day, while cutting down a large tree he slipped and the tree fell on him, crushing his lower leg. The bones were broken in ten places and a large amount of skin had been torn away, so that the bones were exposed. It was the worst accident to a leg that I had ever seen. Any form of plating, or joining, the bones was, of course, completely out since it would have led to infection. Up to recently, amputation would have been the best line of treatment.

This was an extraordinary operation. After cleaning the wound carefully, all the pieces of bone had to be put as near as possible into exact position. But they were very unstable this way; to hold ten pieces together was something which could not be done except by putting the leg into a plaster cast in a bent position and holding it thus until the bones had to some extent become glued together, which would take some weeks. Then a large flap of skin and fat was rotated from the back of the leg to cover the traumatised bone. This left a large area without skin, but grafting can be very successful when placed over muscle. The whole leg was then put into the cast.

The interesting thing happened when the time came to straighten the leg. The man was hypnotised, but it was feared that he might not be deep enough to withstand the pain when the leg was being straightened. I got him to imagine himself going to a football match and just before I took the leg to straighten it, I suggested to him that he was racing down the field, ready to score. At that moment, some change took place in him and he seemed almost to waken from the trance, but then he went under deeply and it was possible to remove the plaster, straighten the leg and get a new cast on. Then he was told to wake up; he looked with amazement at the new plaster on his now-straightened leg. I asked him what had happened when he was running down the field and he replied, 'I was a spectator. I had to break through the crowd to get onto the field.' Then I realised the extraordinary mistake I had made — with a plaster on his leg, of course he would be a spectator. It was an invaluable lesson for me on how vivid the imagination is and how clearly we 'see' things in the subconscious, both in dreaming and in hypnosis.

I am reminded of another 'football' case — a young boy with a large laceration on his leg was admitted. Under hypnosis, I suggested that he was playing football and that he should raise his arm each time he scored a goal. He kept lifting it during the operation, though it did not affect my work on his leg. Afterwards, I asked him whether he remembered anything and to my disappointment, he said he did — he had scored fourteen goals! To my relief, he had no memory of being stitched, even though he had had no local anaesthetic.

Hypnosis can be of use even with 'very bad' subjects — nervous, agitated or terrified people. One case involved a boy who was brought in over the weekend with a broken arm. When I saw him on the Sunday morning, he was waiting for Monday and the return of the radiologist for an X-ray to be taken. After that, he would be put on a waiting list for the fracture to be set. It transpired that the boy had broken his arm previously, at the age of four, and he was terrified of having to stay in hospital, of having an injection, even of having an X-ray.

Now, if hypnosis is used to set a 'greenstick' fracture (an incomplete break), then there is less need to have an X-ray taken beforehand, since the surgeon is able to 'feel' his way. If he is in any doubt at all about the position of the bone, a splint can be applied and an X-ray then taken. On the other hand, using a general anaesthetic to reduce a greenstick fracture means that one cannot stop and continue without the difficulty of having to administer another anaesthetic.

In this case, the boy's fracture was in the middle of the radius (the main bone of the lower arm), split at an angle of 45°. To set this type of fracture, it is necessary to break the bone completely because if the periosteum, or skin of the bone, is intact on one side and ruptured on the other, as a general rule the bone will not set in the correct position. The boy was extremely nervous and a bad subject for hypnosis. Our problem was to set the bone under hypnosis, even though the patient was intensely apprehensive. When hypnotised, he would not go under deeply and even when told he would be completely free of pain, he screwed up his face at the slightest touch to his arm. Eventually, I wakened him to find out what was worrying him so much; I discovered that all he wanted was an assurance that he would be allowed to go home after his arm was fixed. I set his mind to rest on this point and again put him into a trance; still, he would go no deeper. Since manipulating his arm was quite out of the question, I woke him again and told him that I was going to give him an injection for the pain and he would not even feel the touch of the needle. I then rehypnotised him, repeated that he would not feel the injection and gave him 50 mg of pethedine (an amount insufficient to relieve fully the pain of the fractured bone). The operation went smoothly from then on and when the boy was awakened and told that it was all over, his joy was most touching. Without hypnosis, I have no doubt that this boy would have been terrified throughout his stay, perhaps leaving him with a life-long dread of hospitals.

I recall one Christmas period when I had reason to be especially grateful for having hypnosis at my disposal. One day towards the start of the holiday, Mr G____ was admitted to hospital after a head-on collision between his car and another. He was conscious but in a state of shock and with horrific damage done to his face. His injuries included a compound depressed fracture of the frontal bone and compound fractures of both jaws. His face was cut completely through, exposing the mouth and the separated teeth; a large wound entered the hard palate. Added to these were three minor lacerations on his leg.

This was a difficult case, not least from the point of view of giving an anaesthetic: an ordinary tube could not have been passed with safety and a normal anaesthetic would have been fraught with the danger of bleeding from the palate.

When cleaning the wounds, which contained innumerable particles of paint from the car, I found Mr G____ to be a good subject for hypnosis, so I brought him to the theatre with the idea of doing as much as I could at this stage, particularly to control the haemorrhaging. As I progressed, his hypnosis deepened and I was able to elevate the depressed fracture in his skull, wash the loose pieces of bone and put them back in place. I was then able to trace all the minute puncture wounds in the depths of the various lacerations and to pick out the tiny particles of paint; every little depression in each of his face wounds contained at least one piece of glass from the windscreen.

Having treated the skull fracture, I then turned my attention to the compound fracture of the upper jaw, first putting the bones back in position, wiring the teeth and stitching the palate and gums. Then I repaired the lip and side of the face, using the normal methods of plastic surgery. Finally, the wound on the lower jaw and the lacerations on the leg, horribly bruised at the edges, were dealt with.

At the end of the operation, the patient was entirely free from shock, his haemorrhaging was under control and he had no difficulty in getting off the operating table and onto a trolley. The post-hypnotic suggestion, that he would feel no discomfort from his wounds, was totally successful. He was able to take fluids without any pain through a tube into his mouth and with this nourishment he maintained his strength. The operation had taken two and a half hours and was wholly free from pain, with hypnosis the only anaesthetic used.

That same Christmas, on 21 December, a young boy was admitted. A piece of his nose had been bitten off by a dog when he had tried to chase it away from attacking his brother. The following morning, under general anaesthetic, I sutured a pedicle flap (a piece of skin and fat with its blood supply intact) from his arm to his nose and held it in position with a plaster cast around his head and arm — an extremely awkward, but necessary, arrangement. When the operation was over, I gave him his first lesson in self-hypnosis. Soon he was able to distinguish between the trance he could induce and the sleep that would follow it. This practice brought him considerable relief from the difficult position of the cast. On St Stephen's Day, I took off the plaster under hypnosis, removed the sutures and put on a new cast. The boy was able to return to his bed, feeling well and liking the new cast better than the old one.

Curiously, I met this patient again when he was a grown man. He showed no scars nor indeed any trace of the operation, except on his arm — the part from which the skin flap had been taken. He recalled his experiences enthusiastically and was quite surprised that I should remember him so accurately.

Christmas was busy that year — another interesting case arrived on the very day I had completed the 'nose job'. A young man was admitted suffering from osteomyelitis, an inflammation of the bone. He had had this for three days and was in great pain because of the tension created by the pus in his leg. Having taken a cup of tea and eaten half a slice of bread within the past half-hour, the idea of administering a general anaesthetic was immediately ruled out. Plans were made to operate on him at about ten that evening. But the anaesthetist rang to say that the roads were too treacherous with snow for him to be able to travel and could we postpone the operation until the following morning. The patient, however, was suffering greatly. Feeling he might be a suitable case for hypnosis, I put him under and he responded so well that his leg was completely anaesthetised within two to three minutes. To test the genuineness of this, the suggestion was made that he should also feel nothing in his left shoulder. When pricked there with a needle, there was no response — he *was* an excellent subject for hypnosis.

I wanted him in a deep sleep for the operation, so I told him that when he would be lifted off the bed he would go asleep more deeply, that when the trolley went over a bump he would go deeper still and that when he was lifted from the trolley onto the operating table and his leg painted with antiseptic, he would go deeper again. He responded to all these suggestions and when I made the incision over the lower end of the thigh, three inches long, and separated the muscles, he was in a deep hypnotic trance. The pus was drained from the leg and three bore holes made in the femur, or thigh bone, in order to allow all the pus to escape.

The patient looked as if he was in a very deep sleep, so when I suggested to him that his eyes were stuck and he could not open them, I was more than a little taken aback when he opened them and said, 'Of course I can'. He appeared to be completely oblivious of the operation being done on his leg. When finished, I asked him if he could feel a prick on the leg and he said he could; when I looked at his face, I saw that he was completely awake — he knew the operation was over. In his subconscious mind, he obviously associated the return of feeling in his leg with the completion of the operation, yet he had suffered no pain whatever.

Following this, an interesting thing happened. As with most cases of osteomyelitis, further small operations are necessary in the future. Whenever this patient saw me approaching, he developed complete anaesthesia in the affected leg without my even having to hypnotise him.

A sad accompaniment to the Christmas festivities every year is the number of car accidents that occur. Two collision victims arrived one year with identical fractures of the tibia, or shin bone, when their legs had been smashed against the dashboard of their respective cars. The ambulance men had done good work: they had brought the men in quickly, with their legs immobilised in inflated plastic bags. In each case, although the tibia was fractured and displaced, the skin had not been broken and the blood had not clotted, making it easier to set the fractures. The patients were still on trolleys when I suggested hypnosis to them; they agreed, as most people will do under the circumstances. I reduced the fractures, put on plaster casts and, still without pain, had them lifted onto their beds. The bones went back into anatomical position — that is, perfect alignment — and I had only spent a few minutes on each case. The plaster casts did not need to be removed until the bones were completely healed.

Both these cases had an ironic outcome, not from a medical but from an insurance point of view. Each man made a claim and the respective insurance companies paid up. The charge was small, because of the speed with which the men's legs had healed, the small hospital expenses incurred and the minimal amount of time that both were off work.

Throughout this hectic Christmas time, our surgical ward remained a relatively happy place. None of our patients appeared to be in severe pain, if in any pain at all, and there can be no doubt that many operations would have been infinitely more difficult without the aid of hypnosis which, in general surgery, proved absolutely invaluable over this period, as it has done before and since. The advantages, as always, were numerous and resulted in much less suffering on the part of the patients and much greater efficiency and economy on the part of the hospital staff.

One day, a journalist was admitted to the hospital. He was fascinated by the use we were making of hypnosis in surgery and he wrote an article about it which he showed me. Unfortunately, I was not allowed to publish anything about the hospital or the work we were doing there, and the article was never printed. The journalist has died since and now that I am retired, here is his article in full, word for word as he wrote it some 15 years ago:

It is a natural but understandable trait in many people to doubt the veracity of published articles dealing with happenings out of the ordinary and I have no doubt in my mind that having read this article, many people in this country will doubt that such happenings have taken place here in Ireland. However, I can assure my readers that the facts as set out hereunder are true in every detail and can bear the strictest investigation.

I was admitted to a small hospital in a country district in Ireland, where I had my toe amputated. I was in pain after the operation and felt that I might not be able to sleep. I could still feel my toe and I was later to be told that this was called 'phantom pain'. Drugs could easily have been given to me on the night of the operation, but they would not prevent the phantom pains from returning in the morning.

The surgeon who had amputated my toe, when doing nightly rounds, asked me about these pains and told me they could be removed by hypnosis. Being in such acute pain, I agreed to this and he then hypnotised me, suggesting that I would sleep through the night and that I would be free from 'phantom pains'. He awakened me; the pains had gone and I slept quietly and calmly through the night without the aid of drugs.

This was the first time I had any experience of medical hypnosis and, in fact, the first time I had ever heard of hypnosis being used in surgery.

During my stay in hospital, I saw many other patients whom the surgeon treated with hypnosis and I thought to myself that maybe this was the first time that a journalist was lying in hospital amongst patients who were undergoing operations and being helped by hypnosis. So I am writing this article, which may easily be the first of its kind.

Some days after my operation, I was able to move around with the aid of crutches and I went from patient to patient asking them to tell me their stories. Now, for the benefit of readers of this paper, I will give details.

First of these was an intelligent housewife in her early thirties, the mother of four children aged from two to nine years. She had what is known as a femoral hernia. This is a rupture, usually quite small, and necessitating an operation but not of the major class. It was of the utmost importance to this woman that she be kept in hospital for only a short time due to her family obligations. Although her sister-in-law had offered to look after her children, this woman felt that she must be home to see that all was going well, even if she could not do any housework.

She came into hospital in the evening time and that night was given her first lesson in relaxation under hypnosis. The following day she had her operation under hypnosis and a local anaesthetic. She was first of all hypnotised and since she had practised the night before, this only took a few seconds and then the local anaesthetic was given. She had her full breakfast before she went down for her operation and she told me that when she came back from the theatre she felt very well and had a good appetite for her midday dinner. I asked her what she had felt and she told me that she felt the local anaesthetic being given, but it caused no unpleasant sensation of any kind, and that once during the operation she felt something happening, but it caused no pain and in a few moments she was no longer concerned about it. She was completely relaxed and perfectly happy during the whole procedure. She was not completely asleep, just absolutely relaxed and feeling no discomfort.

That evening she got out of bed and walked about and the following day she went home. Seven days afterwards she came back to hospital to have her stitches removed and walked up four flights of stairs to see me. She walked smartly across the ward to the side of my bed, a smiling, happy woman, loud in her praises for a wonderful job well done.

The next patient I interviewed was a 76-year-old retired farm-worker. He looked perfectly happy and contented, sitting in a chair smoking a pipe, oblivious of his surroundings and with a far-away look in his eyes.

I went over to him, fascinated and interested to hear his story too. I said, 'Well, kind sir, and how are you today? You seem very happy in yourself.' He looked at me for a moment and then taking the pipe from his mouth said, 'Beg your pardon sir, did you say something?' I said, 'You look very happy.' Sitting upright in his chair he beamed all over. 'So would you be happy, sir, if you were in my position. Sit down my good man and I'll tell you something.' I sat down. 'I have every reason to be happy,' he started, and showing me a bandaged hand underneath his dressing gown, he continued, 'I am free from pain for the first time in many years. You see, after retiring I had only one pleasure in life — fishing. What more can a man ask from life than to fill his pipe, take out the fishing rod and ramble down the river? That was how I passed my days until fate struck a cruel blow. I thought life, for me, had ended. Instead of fishing, it was pain, pain, pain, all the time. But thank God [he raising his tear-filled, tired old eyes heaven-wards] I am looking forward to many more days fishing down by the riverside now.'

His, certainly, was a remarkable case. When he arrived at the hospital, he had a large growth on his hand; in fact, the whole back of his hand was eaten away. He had been going regularly to doctors to have the bleeding controlled but, finally, when it could not be stopped, he was sent to hospital. He was too old it seems, in the opinion of those who had treated him before he came to hospital, to have an operation. When he arrived at the hospital and had his dressings removed, a large blood vessel commenced to bleed. The surgeon cauterised this with a red-hot electric cautery needle, but first of all he hypnotised him. The patient told me that he remembered being put to sleep, then wakening up, feeling free from pain for the first time in many years and having no recollection of having had his hand burnt.

Later, the growth was removed and now he has a large flap of skin covering the area which is still attached to his body, awaiting the time when it can be separated and sewn finally into place.

This case certainly whetted my appetite and I crossed the ward to a little rosy-cheeked boy of 5-years-old who had attracted my attention. He told me that two bones had been broken in his leg three days previously. It had been very painful and set at that time in a wooden splint. In the hospital, they had set it in plaster of Paris. If anyone had attempted to take the leg out of the wooden splint and put it into plaster without the child being asleep, the first movement would have caused pain and, if the child then had pulled his leg away, the pain would have been agonising and the bones would have moved.

The little boy told me that he had enjoyed having his leg put in plaster and all he remembered was the doctor counting and then telling him that the plaster would have a pleasant feeling. Later, I was told that the bones had been put in position with the greatest of ease, as the leg was relaxed while the child, lying with his eyes closed, was apparently oblivious to anything that was happening. When he was awakened, he smiled and thought the plaster was very nice and comfortable. He was able to move his leg freely the next day and went home the following day, a very happy and contented boy.

The following morning, I was sitting up in bed after breakfast with the thoughts of what I has seen and heard the previous evening surging through my brain, when I saw a tall, fair-haired athletic teenager with a dressing on his nose mount the last few steps leading to my ward. After the usual salutation, he sat down beside my bed and told me his tale of woe. He had been playing soccer the evening before and an opponent's boot had caught him under the nose, breaking it and putting it out of position. On reaching hospital, he was terrified at the thought of being 'needled' and sat there, a bundle of nerves, awaiting the arrival of the surgeon. To his great delight, when the surgeon arrived he hypnotised him and, using considerable pressure, forced his nose back into its correct position; he then set the broken bones with the exception of one small piece which he had to remove. The boy was conscious of everything that was taking place around him, but felt no pain or discomfort. Before leaving me, he confessed that never again would he be afraid to attend hospital with any kind of complaint or injury, as he had enjoyed being treated by hypnosis. I have since seen this boy and I must admit to a job well done.

Again that evening, I saw another patient treated under hypnosis. He had come to hospital to have some fluid taken from his knee. I spoke to him before the surgeon arrived. He had been a patient at the hospital some time before this visit as a result of a motor accident, suffering from severe facial, as well as other, injuries. I saw no visible mark or sign on the man's face. He was of a nervous disposition and told me that he was really terrified of the 'needle'. I do believe that if the man saw anything resembling a needle, he would have passed out.

Eventually the surgeon arrived, hypnotised the subject, inserted a large needle in his knee and drew off the fluid — the whole operation taking only a few moments. When everything was complete, the patient could not be convinced that the operation was over, until he was shown the fluid that had been extracted. He said to me afterwards, 'I have been an awful fool. I had myself worried sick, but never again will that happen.'

When I went to bed that night my mind was in a whirl. I could not think straight. To say that I was amazed at what I had seen and heard from different patients would be putting it mildly. I was stunned. My mind was like a battlefield — hordes of thoughts assailed each other and it remained that way until I found solace in the arms of Morpheus.

The following morning I awoke to the singing of birds. I was happy — happy in the thought that comfort had been brought to so many patients by hypnosis in its application in the surgical ward. There was only one dark cloud in my sky of happiness and that was the fact that I had had to become a patient in a small country hospital to discover this remarkable work being carried out in the place of my birth. There and then, I decided to find out more about hypnosis and to what extent it was used in surgery today and how much it had been used in the past. To my astonishment, this is what I found.

Only a few years before the discovery of anaesthetics, a young Scottish surgeon working in India performed almost 300 major operations under hypnosis, in addition to an enormous number of minor operations. So successful was his work that the government placed a hospital at his disposal. Many of the operations he performed were of the most major kind, even by present-day standards, and he worked not only without anaesthetics, but without blood transfusions or antibiotics — for the first operation was performed 116 years ago.

About this time, anaesthetics were discovered and the work of Dr Esdale, the Scottish surgeon, was forgotten for a hundred years. Now, however, it is being found that while anaesthetics are becoming nearer and nearer to perfection in their reliability and safety, there are many things which anaesthetics cannot do, which hypnosis can accomplish. Hypnosis can lessen the anxiety before an operation and the pain afterwards. It can be used in accident work, for instance in children's fractures, without the almost inevitable delay which is necessary to allow the stomach to empty before giving a general anaesthetic. For painful dressings, repeated anaesthetics may be dangerous, whereas hypnosis usually becomes more successful each time it is applied. Instead of the patient feeling sick after the general anaesthetic, he feels fitter after hypnosis properly performed.

PART II: OVERCOMING CONVENTION

1: Spreading the word

Holding the belief, as I do, that medical curricula should be based on the fact that the vast majority of illnesses spring from the mind, and feeling that insufficient teaching time is allotted to psychosomatic disorders, I have always felt it important to accept invitations to address medical meetings.

The first such request I ever received was from the McCord Zulu Hospital in Durban, where people of various races and colours mixed together in complete harmony and with a sense of fun and humour which I have seldom found equalled anywhere else. I was asked to demonstrate the effects of a short recording I had made on a plastic disc on the subject 'how to relax'; at that time, in 1958, cassette tapes were not in use. About eight doctors attended and they seemed definitely interested in the subject and prepared to cooperate totally. When the record was played each one relaxed deeply, going into at least a light hypnotic trance. As a result of this meeting, I was asked to give a further, clinical demonstration.

Since I had only been practising hypnosis for a few months, I had to search for every available, interesting patient I had treated in that time. Happily, everyone approached was more than willing to participate and there was a full turnout of doctors and other medical staff on the night. I began by recounting the effects of hypnosis on asthma, smoking, childbirth, stammering and other miscellaneous cases I had been treating. The atmosphere of the meeting, however, soon struck me as one of incredulity and even boredom. So, following the dictum, 'If you don't strike oil, stop boring', I said no more and simply started the demonstration by asking all my patients to relax. Their cooperation was so complete that within a few minutes, every one of them was in an hypnotic trance. When requested, one of the doctors brought me a tray of sterilised needles and I pushed one in turn into each of the patients. When the audience saw that no one showed any sign of sensation, the mood changed at once to intense interest.

One patient regressed readily to her early childhood and recalled in detail her first day at school, reeling off the names of all her classmates. The Hospital Secretary was taking down notes in shorthand and she recorded the names. Afterwards, when the volunteers were brought out of their trances, she asked the woman if she could remember her first day at school and the emphatic reply came back, 'Of course I can't'. When asked if she could remember the names of any of her classmates, she had a vague memory of one or two but, beyond that, everything was a blank. Then, to my surprise, the Secretary read out all the names that had been mentioned. The patient was amazed to hear this list of children she had known and now, consciously at least, had forgotten.

After that, questions began to be fired at all the volunteers. One man was asked if it was true his stammer had improved with hypnosis. The reply came back, with no trace of a stammer, that up to the time of his treatment he had been unable to advance in his job because of his impediment. Since he had been cured, he had been involved in an argument with someone in his firm, had won the dispute and, following that, had received promotion.

While all the doctors appeared completely convinced, they nevertheless set me a challenge; they would accept all that I had said about hypnosis on the condition that I would cure three patients of their own choosing. One of the three still stands out in my mind. This woman had had an operation for an untreated tear which had occurred during childbirth; since the operation, she had been unable to empty her bladder without the use of a catheter. She responded immediately to hypnosis, as did the other two patients. However, despite meeting the challenge set me by the other doctors, I was greatly disappointed that none of them felt confident enough in themselves to take up hypnosis and carry it out on their own patients. Hospital staff continually called me in to help with their cases. That was in 1958 and it confirmed to me the necessity of learning how to pass on the art I had acquired.

One upshot of these demonstrations came about when our hospital psychiatrist sent me a message to say that a patient had not responded to any treatment and that he would be grateful if hypnotherapy could be tried. This patient was a Zulu woman, suffering from one of those forms of hysteria whereby she could only walk by contorting her body into exaggerated movements or climb onto her bed with the utmost exertion and grotesque twists. I had heard of a similar case when I was a medical student: a lecturer had told us how, when a man was unable to walk except with his back bent in a curve, he had put him onto an operating table and turned the lever until the patient was forced to stand up straight. But he had never attempted a cure.

My first problem with this woman was one of communication — the only words in Zulu that I knew consisted of a few, largely forgotten sentences which I had used in my work some fifteen years previously. The first thing I wanted to know was whether she could walk normally in a trance. If she could, this would exclude any disease of the nervous system. But how was I to get her into a trance? That was the problem. At that time I always used the word 'sleep', since the only effective hypnosis I had seen in my early studies was that induced by a stage hypnotist who used that word. (Incidentally, this is misleading and patients tended to feel cheated, and not successfully hypnotised, if they did not fall asleep.)

Now the word in Zulu for 'sleep' is *lala*, but *lala* also means 'lie down'. I remembered *lala* from the time I had used it while working in Durban before the war and I kept repeating it to the woman in the most soothing and persuasive voice I could manage. Much to the surprise of the other Zulu patients in the ward, she fell into a trance. Then the next dilemma arose. I wanted her to walk. I remembered the word for this quite easily, appearing as it did on every street corner, warning citizens to walk carefully. Surely, I thought, if I asked her to get up and walk, without an explanation that she was in an hypnotic state, she would immediately open her eyes and come out of the trance. So, although believing that there was no more than a faint hope of success, I used the word *hamba*, meaning 'walk', and the word *lala*, meaning 'sleep', but also meaning 'lie down'. I kept repeating *hamba, lala, hamba, lala* until, to my delight, she got out of bed and started to walk normally, except that her eyes were shut due to the *lala* part of the instruction. Sometimes the right word can spring to mind quite unexpectedly and suddenly I recalled *begamina* — 'look at me' — which I had not heard in fifteen years. So, this time, I said, *lala begamina, lala begamina* — 'sleep, look at me; sleep, look at me'. Remaining in a deep trance, she opened her eyes and walked up and down the corridor; then she ran, the woman in the next bed having told me the word for 'run'. We finally got the patient back into bed and I told her to wake up. She did this without any awareness that she had ever been out of the bed. All the other Zulu women burst out laughing and told her what had happened.

It was clear now that I was dealing with a case of hysteria. The problem remained of finding the cause. I expected that this could be difficult to ascertain, since nothing had emerged during the woman's treatment under a psychiatrist in a very fine hospital. I took a long shot and asked her if she was under *tagati*, the spell of a witch doctor. My beginner's luck was holding out. Yes, she believed she was. But she was also a Christian and she listened intently as I explained, through an interpreter, that what was wrong with her was in her mind, that no Christian could be under the power of an evil spirit. She accepted this and clapped her hands in delight. No further hypnosis was necessary. Both parts of her mind, the conscious and the subconscious, were again in harmony and she returned to her village the next day as though she had never been afflicted.

2: Demonstration at Trinity College, Dublin

Most medical schools have societies run by the students with their usual enthusiasm and when I was first invited to speak to the Biological Association of Trinity College, Dublin (TCD), in the mid-1960s, on medical hypnosis I was determined to put everything I had into the meeting. In order to give a clinical demonstration, I contacted a number of my former patients and all but one accepted my invitation. I did not blame the one who declined, since I agreed with him that he might be compromised by a public demonstration of his severe rheumatoid arthritis. The Examination Hall, the venue for the meeting, is on the right side of TCD's main quadrangle as one comes in the Main Gate and is one of the most striking classical interiors in Ireland. It was crowded the night I was to speak and the atmosphere was one of intense interest and anticipation. I am happy to say that this feeling remained throughout the evening and my brother later told me that when he had been sitting among the students he had overheard conversations to the effect that some of those present could scarcely believe what they had seen. Being a scrupulously honest man, he had to tell them that he was my brother and that it was all true.

Patients were shown in rapid succession and I will describe several in order to illustrate the mood of the proceedings.

Mr G____ is one of the few people one is likely to meet in a lifetime who is accurately described as 'one of nature's gentlemen'. Everything about him was honourable and generous. He had been a pilot in the pre-RAF Army Flying Corps during the First World War, surviving many missions in a tiny bi-plane, and now, in his old age, was a house agent. He had once done me a very good turn and I longed for the opportunity to repay him.

One day, he was wheeled into hospital following a severe car accident. He was an enormous man physically and was wearing an equally enormous overcoat under which his arm was in an abnormally contorted position. His shoulder appeared to be dislocated. It was impossible to tell what internal injuries he might have sustained without cutting off his coat and jacket — a procedure bound to cause fierce pain and, in any case, possibly dangerous. I stopped the wheelchair in the corridor and felt the shoulder. In some cases, it is difficult to tell if there is a dislocation, in others it is obvious — in this case it was obvious. Even without a dislocated shoulder, it is virtually impossible to take off a heavy overcoat when the owner cannot be lifted, and now it could be done only at the expense of causing the patient extreme agony. And even then, the danger remained of the uncertainty as to whether or not the ribs were broken, the lungs damaged or the stomach full, thus making the administration of a general anaesthetic impossible.

Fortunately, Mr G____ was an ideal hypnotic subject: he was intelligent, in grave need, cooperative and had humility. Of greater importance, we trusted each other completely. Within two or three minutes he was deeply relaxed. With the first manoeuvre, his arm slipped easily into its socket; after that, the coat and jacket were removed without difficulty. On examination, it was found that his ribs were broken, that one of his lungs had collapsed and that he was bleeding profusely into the space between the lung and the chest wall. It took only an equally simple suggestion for him to be freed from discomfort, for the blood to be aspirated, or drawn out, and the lung expanded. When the demonstration at Trinity was over, the students crowded around Mr G____, full of questions. When asked how much pain he had suffered when being treated, the old airman replied, 'It was no more than a fly taking off.'

Another of my former patients at the TCD meeting that night was Mr S____. He had been brought to our hospital as a young boy, about 10 years old, by the Christian Brothers who ran a school nearby. The Brothers said that it was the worst case of asthma they had ever seen and that the boy's education was erratic owing to his frequent absences from school. They explained that he could not run as much as three steps without bringing on an attack. I have never seen a case so difficult in the years that have passed since I first saw Mr S____; in fact, his very survival was threatened.

Whereas most children of his age obtain relief almost immediately with hypnotherapy, this boy came to see me week after week, month after month, until he eventually learned to take away his attacks unaided. It was important that the medical students at the TCD meeting should realise the severity of this patient's previous condition and so two of the Christian Brothers had agreed to come along and answer questions. Then with his permission, and to drive the point home irrefutably, I regressed Mr S____ to a former attack. His lungs went into spasm as they used to. Students drew around him with their stethoscopes to listen to his chest wheezing. I then asked Mr S____ to take his attack away. He sat down, counted to six, relaxed with ease and his spasm went. This boy later took up running seriously and has been successful in his chosen profession.

Mr H____ was working with a turf-cutting machine when his arm became entangled and twisted until it was wrenched off, just below the shoulder joint, leaving only a few inches of bone, with the muscle attached but with the rest of the flesh missing. Up until recent years, the standard operation in such cases has been amputation at the shoulder joint. Now, with antibiotics, skin grafting and sophisticated artificial limbs, we try to salvage the stump.

After the operation, Mr H____ had the sensation of the arm being still present and agonisingly painful, as though being twisted and burned. These sensations of a limb, or even a finger, being painfully present after an amputation are known as 'phantom pains'. When a surgeon does his rounds the morning after an operation list, he is often told 'I can still feel my foot and the pain is unbearable'. He can do one of three things — the first two are routine, the third belongs to tomorrow's world.

First, he can reassure the patient which, in itself, has a beneficial effect. The patient accepts fully the truth that his pain sensation will lessen while, at the same time, he will be able to bear it better. The second is the giving of pain-killers or tranquillisers, which deaden the pain slightly and make it easier to bear. The third is hypnosis.

Mr H____ was lying in agony, having lost a limb which the previous day he had been using normally. It was explained to him that these pains diminish in the course of time and in order to alleviate his mental anguish, he was reassured that he would be looked after financially, how compensation would be paid and how he could be trained for some other kind of work. I had little hope of being able to fit an artificial arm, since I had never before had to deal with such a badly torn shoulder.

Phantom pains are due to the subconscious mind failing to grapple with, and adjust to, a new situation. Having no computed information, it allows the sensory part of the brain to register each electrical impulse that travels up the severed nerves to the brain. The brain does not know what to do with these impulses and it registers them as coming from the parts which have been severed. By reaching the subconscious mind, we can get it to realise that these sensations should not be transmitted. Phantom pains, to the sufferer, are no different than ordinary ones. They feel just as 'real'. Thus the highest ethical rules of medicine still apply: to treat the root cause while, at the same time, treating the symptoms. As Mr H____ wanted desperately to be relieved of his pain, hypnosis was used. In the hospital atmosphere of dependence and trust, he relaxed easily. His subconscious mind accepted the fact that there was no limb present and nothing to be gained from transmitting pain sensations. Within two minutes, he was out of his agony and the pain did not recur.

Mr H____'s stump, now covered with skin, had become so strong in the intervening years that one athletic medical student who came forward to examine it at the TCD meeting was unable to hold it down by its owner's side. How much of this would have happened without treatment reaching the subconscious mind I do not know. But the fact that he accepted a post-hypnotic suggestion, following the disappearance of the phantom pains, which enabled him to be free from discomfort also allowed him to move the limb, thereby preventing adhesions from forming and developing the muscles of the stump at the same time. He was eventually fitted with a most ingenious artificial arm and great credit must be given to the instrument-makers who carried out this brilliant work in the National Rehabilitation Centre, for they had contrived a limb which had an elbow that bent and a hand that opened and closed, all controlled by the movements of Mr H____'s small, but powerful stump.

I have already mentioned the case of Mr G____, who was admitted to hospital with horrific facial injuries following a severe car crash (see p. 28). The TCD students examined the scars on his forehead over the right eye, where the frontal sinus had been driven in. This bone had been taken out, washed to remove the road dirt, then replaced and the wound stitched. There had also been a fracture of the skull behind the eye (fortunately, the eye itself had escaped injury), which went down through the bones of the face, splitting the palate wide open. In addition, his lower jaw had a compound fracture and his leg some ragged wounds.

Mr G____'s whole operation was performed over a two and a half hour period without a local anaesthetic and no pain was felt. It created considerable interest at the time, not only because of the ease with which extensive plastic surgery had been carried out but also because of the effect of the post-hypnotic suggestion used to free the patient from later discomfort. In spite of his upper jaw being wired and his lower jaw having a compound fracture, he was never short of nourishment in the form of liquid food. On the ninth day after the operation he returned home, his wounds completely healed. I saw him two years later, when his case for compensation was being settled, and in all that time he had never felt any discomfort.

Another case I discussed at the TCD meeting was that of Mrs D____, who had suffered extensive burns when an oil stove had blown up in her face. She needed frequent dressings for these and in order to ease the pain, she was taught self-hypnosis. Each time the wounds were to be dressed, she would lie down and put herself into a deep hypnotic trance, fully conscious but with total anaesthesia. When the dressings were complete, she refused to rouse herself until she had had at least half an hour of lying in a state of total tranquillity.

Most of the other cases demonstrated at the TCD meeting were similar to those already described. They merely underlined the advantages of hypnosis for anaesthesia as a method of treatment which does not entail the necessity of an empty stomach, can be induced quickly and results in a reduction of suffering. As regards economy, the savings in hospital personnel and resources were immense. The students were fascinated, particularly by the young boy who had had part of his nose bitten off by a dog *(see p. 29)* and by several of the car-crash victims who recounted how post-hypnotic suggestion had helped in dispelling their consequent fears of driving, or of being driven, after the accident.

The effect of the demonstration was an acceptance by three Dublin medical schools and a post-graduate school for courses in hypnotherapy, with the offer of full cooperation from the deans and registrars. The ensuing classes produced some interesting results. One student, who had failed his anatomy and physiology exams in the College of Surgeons, volunteered to train in increased ability of study and recall; in the next examination, he took first place in those subjects which he had failed so ignominiously before. Another student, who had seen the demonstration but was unable to come to the classes, had the following story to tell. He was attending a teaching round in hospital when the class was brought to an oxygen tent where a woman lay gasping for breath, with a severe asthmatic attack. The professor told the class that there was nothing more that could be done for her and that she would probably die soon.

Now, this student was one of those medics who are both conscientious and fearless — the type that so often make trouble and so often find a cure. When the class was over, he went to the professor and asked permission to use hypnosis on the woman. With the professor's agreement, he went back to the woman, never having hypnotised anyone before, but seeing the possibility of saving a life, did what he felt he had to do and tried. He found a ready response, typical of someone in an asthmatic attack about to die. When all hope for her life had gone, he managed to stop the attack and within a few days the woman was discharged from hospital.

3: Lecture at University College, Dublin

On 2 December 1982, I was asked to give a lecture to the Medical Society of University College, Dublin (UCD), which, like the Biological Association of TCD, is the medical students' own organisation within the Dublin campus of the National University. I was one of five people who had been invited to speak on 'alternative medicine' and my subject was, of course, hypnotherapy. I accepted the invitation, but not on the basis that hypnotherapy is alternative medicine. It is rapidly being accepted as an essential part of medical training in many parts of the world and it is my hope that, in time, its teaching will be universal. I will here reproduce the beginning of the lecture I gave to this meeting:

Medicine has just emerged from the age of mysticism to that of the body-snatchers, when anatomy was put on to a scientific basis. Since then, anatomy has been accurately taught and physical-ailment consequences scientifically treated. But the dead bodies did not contain minds and, ever since then, we have been teaching, most exclusively, how to treat physical conditions, when most illnesses are psychosomatic — they spring from the mind. Unless we emerge from the body-snatching era, in which we have remained too long, we can only treat adequately the minority of patients who come to us for help.

If any doctor were to practise without using antibiotics, he would be struck off the Medical Register — many of his patients would die unnecessarily without their use. Yet, if one who had used hypnosis were faced with the choice of whether he should give up antibiotics or hypnosis, he would be faced with a difficult choice. At first sight it might appear that antibiotics are, beyond question, the more important. Yet antibiotics, unlike hypnosis, can touch only a small proportion of human suffering.

When penicillin was first discovered, a small batch was sent to the north of England for experimental use. No one seemed to believe in it and it lay there, unused. Consequently, even though a relatively junior surgeon, I was allowed to make the first trial and I injected it into a septic hip joint. The result was dramatic and I have used antibiotics ever since and hypnotherapy for only a little over half that time. I believe that shutting one's eyes to the use of hypnotherapy is as unscientific as the shutting of one's eyes to the possible uses of penicillin; because if they are closed to the fact that there is access to the subconscious mind, we will continue to treat patients symptomatically with such things as tranquillisers, sleeping tablets and bronchial dilators, instead of aiming at curing the root cause of complaints.

You know, and I think you will agree one hundred per cent, that the nervous system is composed of the voluntary and the autonomic, and that the latter part is controlled by the subconscious mind. What is more important is that we have access to the subconscious mind and, if we do not accept this fact and make use of it, then we are cowboys. What's more, cowboys without lassoos — for if we cannot catch this evasive beast, we will continue to see the appalling and unnecessary incidence of suffering and death from readily curable psychosomatic conditions.

Soon, you will be the custodians of the nation's health. But, tonight, when all the doctors' surgeries are shut except for emergency work, there will be, throughout this country, many organisations at work to which people have turned rather than to orthodox medicine — organisations practising yoga, Silva Mind, Christian Science, lay hypnosis, acupuncture, chiropractice, osteopathy and homeopathy.

This evening, you are due to hear four other short lectures. One is on chiropractice — the word comes from *chiro* meaning 'hands' and *practice* — 'to do'. Another is on osteopathy, which is practised in the belief that the skeletal structure of the body is the foundation for health. An acupuncturist will then speak on this ancient practice, founded on the belief that there are various pathways in the body and that by reaching them, many illnesses can be cured. A homeopath will give a lecture on his subject, which is based on the belief that if we use in minute quantity something which with a larger dose would cause illness, then this fractional dose will bring about a cure.

You are all looking very glum, so I'm going to tell you a story which I hope will amuse you. One fine summer's morning a young woman, who had just passed her exams in psychiatry, got up early to go for a walk down by the sea. The water looked tempting and, since no one was about, she took off her clothes and went for a swim. But on the same morning, a young man had also got up early and was out for a walk on the cliffs. When he saw a bundle of clothes on the beach and, out in the sea, the head of the young doctor, the 'divil' got into him and he sat down beside the bundle of clothes. The girl kept swimming around and around until she could stand the cold no longer. She came out and, flinging her arms across her chest, walked toward the young man. While she was doing so, she kicked something and, to her delight, picked up a frying pan. Holding it in front of her, she walked up to him, looked him straight in the eyes and said, 'I'm a psychiatrist and I know what you're thinking, and you didn't know that I would find a frying pan on the way out of the sea.' He looked her straight in the eyes and replied, 'I am not a psychiatrist, but I know what you are thinking — you think there's a bottom in that frying pan.'

You are looking happier now and I hope you are in agreement that, if we are going to fulfil the highest ethics of the medical profession and the Hippocratic Oath, we must realise that we do not possess all knowledge and that we must continue to move out of the era of the body-snatchers into a wider, more exciting profession where we treat people who have minds. I shall tell you about some of the cases that I have seen within the past ten days. If anyone wishes to verify the accuracy of any of the accounts of these cases, he is welcome to do so and I shall put him in touch with the patients concerned . . .

4: When Television looked for Entertainment

In 1967, I received a request from Radio Telefís Éireann (RTE, the Irish national broadcasting service) that I help prepare a five-minute session on medical hypnosis to be included in a quarter-hour programme involving various hypnotists. I accepted, but only on the proviso that the entire programme be purely medical, to which the broadcasting authorities agreed.

The medical profession is bound by many ethical rules, some written and some unwritten, but all important. In the years since this episode occurred, the rules have been somewhat relaxed, but in those days no doctor in competitive practice was allowed to reveal his name in any medium if it would help in building up a practice, unless the withholding of his name might do the public a disservice and outweigh the importance of anonymity.

The Irish Medical Association (IMA, as it was then) was most helpful, as it and the British Medical Association have always been. It agreed that hypnotherapy should not be left to those outside the medical profession and that we should make more use of it. The IMA agreed to the television project provided that we observed two golden rules: firstly, that no doctor's name be mentioned nor that of any hospital, and, secondly, that any correspondence sent to the television studios for any doctor should be returned to the sender. It was added, as an amicable gesture, that these precautions having been taken, should one's name be mentioned accidently, it would be understood and need give no cause for worry. As this was not a live programme, these rules gave no trouble.

The TV cameras and equipment were brought to the hospital and the director gave us to understand that he had been given an ample budget, which, in the event, he scarcely had to draw upon as no one asked for any payment. The aim of the producers was to make a gripping programme which would entertain. Our aim was to advance knowledge of hypnotherapy. But we were all united in the ambition to produce a programme that would hold the audience's attention. Much would depend on what happened in the hospital on that particular day. As it turned out, there was no shortage of cases to demonstrate and, in fact, double the amount of time available could have been filled with fast-moving enthralling action. Later, the producers did obtain permission to extend the programme.

Mr B____ was one of the first. He was a young man of twenty who had been admitted with an abscess on his forehead which was causing concern because of its proximity to his eye. He was waiting for an operation. When asked if he would be willing for it to be lanced under hypnosis, while being filmed, his face lit up at the offer and he grinned from ear to ear. Struck by this bit of luck at the start, we asked why he was so pleased. It turned out that he had once had a broken nose, which I had set under hypnosis, and knowing that he would not have to miss a meal, would feel no pain during the operation and no sickness afterwards, in addition to appearing on television, he was more than willing to participate.

As eager a performer as this young man was, our real star was a woman called Mrs M____. She was a sterling person, of a kind that one is fortunate to meet once or twice in a lifetime. She had worked in a munitions factory in London throughout the war and had been injured during the blitz. A series of operations had followed. It sometimes happens that strain has the effect of causing trouble in the thyroid; sometimes the thyroid itself is the cause of the strain. Mrs M____ had developed a condition known as thyrotoicosis, whereby the goitre enlarges slightly, the eyes bulge, the hands shake and the heart beats faster, while the products of the overactive gland also force the body to burn up fats and tissues. Added to the seventeen operations performed on her initial injury, Mrs M____ had had her thyroid gland partially removed. It was after this that she had returned to Ireland. She was in an acute surgical ward and, despite the pressure for beds, had been there for five years. She was a very observant and alert lady; every movement of every patient was stored by her brain, enabling her to tell a house surgeon, quicker than he could look around him, all that was happening in the ward.

At this time, it was one of her two crippled legs that was giving the most trouble. After her eighteenth operation, this useless leg had to be amputated. On the evening round the house surgeon, who was walking in front of me into the ward, saw her apparently lifeless and thought her failing heart had not stood up to the operation. But she was far from dead. She soon became as active as ever but, when the other leg started giving trouble, the anaesthetist declared that she could not withstand another amputation. Mrs M____, however, was determined to live and, further, not to become a burden to anyone. The second leg was amputated under deep hypnosis, with the aid of a local anaesthetic. How can the human mind control a body with no legs, a bad heart and a thyroid condition? The answer could be found by talking to Mrs M____.

Like most of their colleagues, the reporters on this RTE television programme were people trained to seek out the truth and to discover discrepancies, and they have a public who are equally interested in hearing facts, be they new ones or ones which expose falsehood. Mrs M____ revelled in being under fire from such people. She recounted to them how she had undergone eighteen operations under general anaesthetic, but that when her second leg had been amputated under hypnosis, she had been able to return to the ward without pain, had asked for a good meal and eaten it with a fine appetite. She explained what phantom pains were and how they had followed her first amputation, but that she had been free from all such discomforts after the second. The reporters would not let her go: they asked her what she would do were she to need a further operation. With her gleaming, exophthalmic eyes, she rose to this with all the joy of a trout rising to a mayfly. She explained how, after the one done under hypnosis, she had lost all fear of operations; that if she were to have another one, she would no longer have to wait in apprehension and hunger, and would have no sickness and pain when she woke. She knew also that she would have no post-operative discomfort and that even her stitches could be removed without her feeling any sensation at all.

Mrs M____, incidentally, was at this time pressing the local council to give her a house built to her special requirements and, with an admirable sense of responsibility toward the public purse, they looked at this frail, elderly lady who had no legs, bulging eyes and tremulous hands, and they temporised. As the years progressed, however, they did eventually build a house for her where she lived for some years. In this tiny, immaculately kept home, any visitor was sure to be handed a cup of tea and something cooked by Mrs M____ herself.

Mr S____, the young man who had suffered so severely from asthma (see p. 42), appeared on the programme as a guest and his demonstration of the way in which he could relax himself and relieve his attacks was most effective. There had been a plan to broadcast the sounds of his breathing, but this had to be jettisoned for no matter how strongly the suggestion was given that he was frightened or his chest in spasm, the former loud, piping noise could no longer be induced. The sounds made now were only those of a normal, mild attack.

As there were more cases than could be fitted into even this fast-moving programme, time had to be allowed for one to be shown that would help to give credibility to a subject that needed it. I decided to ring a Christian Brother and ask him if he would go into the studios the next day. He readily agreed. He had been admitted with a friend late one night, both having been involved in a car crash in which their faces were badly torn. I had been working all day and did not feel that I could easily continue to work through the night. The decision I made was to operate on the Christian Brother's face at once, under hypnosis. The other, I would operate on under general anaesthetic in the morning. It is difficult, if not impossible, to repair a badly lacerated face using a local anaesthetic, since so much has to be injected into so many different places. If the surgeon finds pocket after pocket filled with blood and dirt, he can often wish that he had never started in the first place.

The Christian Brother on whom I had operated went into the RTE studio as promised and described how he felt no pain while his enormous facial lacerations were being stitched under hypnosis. Then, when the nurses came around in the morning to give out breakfast, he was more than ready to eat as he felt so well. He was able to get up, while his unfortunate friend, his face covered with blood-soaked bandages, was kept fasting in preparation for his operation.

And so, with these cases and many more, the first documentary film of hypnosis in the surgical ward of a hospital was broadcast in November 1967. RTE presented us with a video of the programme which, on an interest/cost ratio, must have been one of the least expensive programmes ever made. Without any special expenses, a programme had been produced double the originally intended length. Something else was done — it was shown twice, a thing that had not happened previously on Irish television.

PART III: THE APPLICATION

1: Pain

Without pain we would die. Pain tells us there is something wrong. There is very little understood about pain by the average person, but knowledge of its mechanism and the method of controlling it can mean the difference between happiness and living in agony. If the subconscious mind has not fully understood that the pain has been investigated and everything has been done for it, then it will continue to allow the pain sensations to be felt at the maximum degree. If, on the other hand, the subconscious mind has accepted the fact that the pain has been treated and that there is no more to be done for the moment, then it is capable of cutting off the sensation of pain or reducing it.

Let us take a couple of simple examples. A bee-keeper loves his bees and likes working with them. When he is stung, he treats it as a triviality and brushes the bees aside. But someone who is afraid of bees and gets stung will feel the pain intensely. Or take the person who is picking blackberries and gets a thorn stuck in his finger; he pulls it out and thinks no more of it. The same person could go to the dentist and feel intense pain with an injection, yet the needle is only a fraction of the size of the thorn. In one case, he was relaxed; in the other, he was tensed. The lesson here is that if we relax and remain relaxed, while at the same time knowing for certain that all is being done for us that can be done, then we can either lose pain completely or, at least, be better able to bear it.

There are two types of pain — physical and psychosomatic. These two are more commonly mixed together and it is a help to know what proportion comes from either source, though in any case both can respond. Migraine, for example, is probably psychosomatic. It is brought on by unresolved conflicts in the mind. It will respond to hypnosis if we allow the conflicts to disappear. This may be a big job, but once the mind is at ease and the true facts are absorbed by the subconscious, then we are free. We no longer feel the intense pain over the eyes which comes when the constricted blood vessels dilate.

In the case of arthritis, I once examined a man before he went on a mountain-climbing trip to India. His knees were as rough and as bad from arthritis as I have ever seen. Yet he felt no pain. Why was this? It is difficult to say, except that he had always wanted to do this and was resolved to have fun at the same time. His attitude of mind eliminated his pain. Other people, however, can suffer terrible pain from a small degree of arthritis. I myself was almost crippled until I tried hypnosis and the relief was immense. Now, nine years later, I can still dig in the garden which I could not possibly have done before.

The power of the subconscious mind is best illustrated by considering what happens during the hours of sleep. When we are asleep, the subconscious mind is in complete control. If a noise occurs that is of any importance, the subconscious has the job of waking us up. However, if the noise is of no consequence, the same subconscious mind functions by ensuring that we are not disturbed. This may sound like over-simplification, but it is not. We all know how the crying of a baby can wake its parents, even when that sound is barely audible. The rattling of a window, on the other hand, might pass entirely unnoticed, unless we are annoyed and angry about it, in which case it can actually keep us awake. Many people unafraid of thunder will sleep through a thunderstorm. It is totally an attitude of mind.

When the subconscious mind is in harmony with the conscious, unhelpful stimuli are prevented from reaching the conscious. This is true whether the stimulus is the pollen which causes asthma, that sensation in the back which produces discomfort or noises in the ear which may resemble the roar heard in a railway station. In our modern civilisation, we tend to turn at the least problem to aspirin, tranquillisers or any form of pain-killer we can lay our hands on. All these drugs have certain adverse side-effects and none is completely free from danger. Remember, too, that any pill that will dull pain will also dull the mind. If we train ourselves in mind control, however, we can eliminate unnecessary pain or, at least, bear it more easily, so avoiding the dangerous side-effects and risks of addiction inherent in many pain-killers.

Let us consider the subject of cancer. When a person is relaxed, pain is much easier to bear; if he is tensed, alarming doses of pain-killers may have to be administered. If the person is to be told that he has cancer, and it is sometimes very necessary to do so, it is essential that the person in charge is sympathetic and knows what he is doing. Assuming these conditions exist, we have got to get the person to relax as much as possible and to accept that all is being done to help. This relaxation may be deepened as far as possible, using hypnotic techniques or any others that work. Books are available that tell you how to relax and are well worth reading, but perhaps the greatest technique of all is that of one human being talking to another. I have produced cassettes, one called *The Art of Relaxation* and another on *Conquering Pain*, both of which, I am told, afford relief.

While many of the conditions described in this book may only apply to some readers, pain is likely — indeed, certain — to be experienced by all of us. So it is worth everyone's while to acquire some basic techniques which will enable us to gain at least a degree of control over pain and, in many cases, relief from a condition which is making life more or less intolerable. The method I have used thousands of times with patients is described on p. 119; to me it is the most practical method and the one with which I have had most success over 30 years of hypnotherapy. Examples of the efficacy of this relaxation method are given throughout the text — examples of ordinary people, not gurus or mystics, helping themselves through controlling their own minds and tapping into that enormous reservoir of energy in the subconscious. Anyone can do it — it just needs a genuine resolve to face your specific problem and then a little application.

2: Painless Childbirth

Probably the most successful role in which hypnotherapy can be used in everyday life is in painless childbirth. There are two main reasons for this — it is natural and it can be a very pleasant event. When the baby is finally in the mother's arms, she should be very happy. Furthermore, children born with a relaxed mother are infinitely fitter. This is one subject we are all involved in, since we are all born and most of us will take part in reproducing.

Boxers, bee-keepers and wrestlers may seem irrelevant in this context, but think for a moment of the excruciating pain of the skin being ripped open from a cut above the eye, yet the boxer, for example, is only concerned about the blood that flows down and prevents him seeing; the bee-keeper gets stung numerous times, yet he simply knocks his attackers to one side; the wrestler whose joints appear to be almost ripped apart is relatively oblivious of the pain. A mother, on the other hand, has all the anticipation of receiving a healthy baby at the end of her labours and will have all the instinctive love and care for it. Now, it is in this condition that hypnosis works best.

If women were to have their babies when they were young, their bodies more supple and before their minds were filled with horror stories about painful births, they would have them relatively easily. But while this is true, most women have their babies when they are slightly older. Yet they can still have them painlessly or almost so if they learn the secret of relaxation from the start.

Firstly, it is important to know something about the body — how certain muscles relax while others contract, leaving free passage for the baby. The uterus is under the control of the subconscious mind and so we have nothing to do with it except to give it reinforcement when the time comes for the delivery. With this knowledge and by practising relaxation techniques from the time she becomes pregnant, a woman can be in great fettle for the birth itself. At the start of the pregnancy, she can try controlling morning sickness; then, having practised relaxing for the best part of nine months, she can relax the relevant muscles when the baby is being born and push it through a wide-open door — nature will tell her when to do so. If you are fully relaxed, every muscle that should relax *will* relax.

One thing should be made clear, however: while there is a much higher percentage of women who actually enjoy the delivery of their babies with hypnosis, there is a smaller number who feel some discomfort and a tiny number who find no relief. If you are one of the latter or if there is some abnormality and an epidural block is given, you can still use hypnosis to relax during the whole procedure. Many other advantages can also be gained from relaxing.

To give one example of the many cases I have come across — a woman who came to my Smoking Clinic had an extraordinary story to tell. She had had three babies, each weighing over 10 lb (4.5 kg) and each delivered by forceps. She was, according to herself, the worst patient the hospital ever had. She was strongly advised by her doctor not to have any more children, but she had a great longing for one more child. So she changed doctors and went to another man who advised her to try relaxation. She bought the cassette *Towards Painless Childbirth* and practised with it ardently. When the time came for the delivery, she was so relaxed that she lay in hospital actually enjoying the natural birth of the baby, which again weighed over 10 lb.

It was in 1932. I remember it clearly for I was delivering women under the most appalling conditions in the slums of Dublin. I had the women pulling on towels tied to the end of their beds and many were in the first stages of labour. I was a young medical student and though I had won a prize in obstetrics (midwifery), I did not know that a woman should not force downwards until the second stage is reached. I carried this memory with me until I started work in Guernsey in the 1950s. At that time, Dr Grantby Dick Reid had started his work on natural childbirth. This transformed my approach to midwifery. I bought his book, but not having time to read it I lent it to a patient. The result was dramatic: she relaxed when I said 'relax', she pushed when I said 'push', she appeared to be almost free from pain and there was much less bleeding. I decided to try this out on other patients, so I got a few more copies of the book and distributed them, with similar results. I did not know then that what Dr Reid was advocating was simply a method of hypnosis; he did not understand it either and, though he spoke with honesty, he met with tremendous opposition within the medical profession. Yet it was largely due to his work, I believe, that a new approach was taken to childbirth.

In 1960, the obstetrics department of the Irish Medical Association (IMA) invited the gynaecologist Mr Evans of Cardiff to talk on his use of hypnosis in delivery by Caesarian section; this technique involved one-third of all his cases. I had been invited to talk after Mr Evans and I related my own, similar experiences with hypnosis and childbirth. It was following this lecture that the various psychoprophylaxis clinics opened in Ireland, to teach women about natural childbirth. At least I believe that it was as a result of this talk to the IMA. Many other teaching centres have since opened and most of them are doing good work, but I feel that if they knew the value of self-hypnosis they would do even better.

3: Asthma

There are minute muscles in the microscopic branches of the lungs' bronchial tubes. These muscles regulate the passage of gases in and out of the bloodstream. Their lining is so thin that oxygen breathed in from the air passes freely through it into the blood and waste gases (carbon dioxide, for example) pass, just as freely, from the blood out into the air. These tiny muscles also contract naturally from time to time to keep out unwanted substances.

It is the tiny muscles in the lungs that appear to be at fault in asthmatic cases. They go into spasm when they do not need to and they do this because a person has become hypersensitive to something. Frequently, asthma is divided into cases which are psychosomatic and those that are considered physical in origin. But, in a sense, all cases are psychosomatic because if the person reacts to physical things, such as pollen in the air, he must be hypersensitive.

Breathing is an automatic process. The conscious mind can regulate it to a certain extent — we can decide to go out for a walk or to open a window to get more air, or we can decide to breathe more or less deeply, even to hold our breath, when we want to. But it is the subconscious mind that regulates the incredibly delicate and infinitely complex exchange of gases within the lungs. This mechanism is entirely outside our conscious control; it is automatic and involuntary, run by our internal computer system of sense-impression and memory. The muscles that go into spasm during an asthmatic attack are thus completely under the control of the subconscious mind. Fortunately, they are easily reached.

CHILDREN
A typical asthmatic case may develop as follows. A child is sent away from home because his mother is having another baby. He does not understand why he has to go and stay with his granny in the country. He may believe that something is wrong at home and this will make him anxious and unhappy. In the country, he may come into contact with pollen for the first time. Now, pollen is not harmful to the average person, but to anyone under stress or tensed up, everything in the body tends to react quickly or to

over-react. Pollen is a foreign substance to such a person and the tiny muscles in the lungs contract, or go into spasm, in order to keep it out. Thus, an asthmatic attack is brought on. The child cannot catch his breath, he is frightened and his fright makes the attack worse. If he were happy and relaxed, the pollen would have had no effect.

Next time he encounters pollen, because the subconscious is dealing with inaccurately computerised feelings, he suffers another attack. Because this whole mechanism is outside the control of his conscious mind and reasoning, any time the boy goes to the country, or even meets the family with whom he was unhappy, even without the pollen being present the situation can throw his lung muscles into spasm again. Or perhaps he may be out in the country when he comes into contact with something else which makes breathing slightly difficult, such as fog or dust or smoke, or maybe he is subject to some indefinable fear, such as an unfamiliar sound or a strange animal; any of these things may become just one more way in which an asthmatic attack is triggered.

We can take such a child and test him for allergies, by making small scratches in the skin and then rubbing various substances into them. In this way, we can find out which ones he reacts to and then immunise him against them. But more often than not, we find there are others against which he has no immunity. Thus the results of this kind of treatment are often disappointing. Other orthodox ways of attacking asthma include prescribing drugs to try and paralyse the tiny muscles responsible for the lungs' spasms and the administering of cortisone to reduce their reactions. Each week, new asthmatic preparations come on the market and are advertised to doctors by mail shot with monotonous regularity.

In my view, and having dealt with many asthmatic cases, there is one factor common to all allergies and that factor is subconscious fear. While it may be useful, at least until a patient is over the immediate attack, to give drugs and hormones, it is the cause that must be found and cured. It is only in the reaching of the subconscious mind, the erasure of the erroneous information stored there and its replacement with the true facts, that a cure will be effected. In the meanwhile, a patient can control his asthma by learning the methods of relaxation that will give freedom from attack.

There is a small but significant percentage of people who do not believe that hypnosis is morally acceptable. This group includes many of the finest people one is likely to encounter on this earth and it is for their benefit especially that I again take great pains to distinguish between self-hypnosis and the hypnosis that takes over (or is believed to take over) the mind of another. I once knew a man who stated flatly that he was against anti-apartheid, believing that it was the same as apartheid. Self-hypnosis is, in the most important of ways, the direct opposite of hypnosis since it is a means of gaining control over *one's own* mind in order to free *oneself* from harmful conceptions that may control or influence it. With self-hypnosis, we do not go to sleep and the conscious mind keeps a watching brief over the subconscious, allowing any suggestions that we consider undesirable to be refused.

To those totally opposed to any kind of hypnosis, there are two things I would like to suggest. First, that if you wish to help someone with asthma, especially a child, and you can promote in him a sense of love and security, and help him find within himself the power to face his underlying worries and dilemmas — you will find that this is the most valuable help you can offer. In this kind of situation, it is of tremendous benefit to speak loving words of encouragement to a child at night, just before he or she drops off to sleep. These words, at such a receptive time, tend to sink in deeply and help the child to become a different, stronger and better equipped person. The process helps to restore harmony between the conscious and the subconscious mind, the lack of such harmony being at the root of the trouble.

The second thing I would like to suggest is that if a person relaxes and puts all thoughts out of the mind as far as in his power, except those which he wishes to sink deeply into the mind, both parts of the mind can be brought into the desired harmony. In an asthmatic's case, the spasm in the bronchial muscles can be rapidly relieved and the body's glands enabled to produce the correct quantities of hormones required.

There is nothing mystical or mysterious going on in these processes. Some people might call them forms of hypnosis or mind control; if they are, then so is a lullaby.

A certain hospital once offered me the opportunity of seeing what I could do through the use of hypnosis to help children who had been admitted for asthmatic conditions for an average of six months and who had been undergoing intensive orthodox treatments. One recent arrival, a little girl, was suffering from both asthma and eczema. Under hypnosis, it was revealed that her first attack occurred when she went alone into a loft in the dark and suddenly found that something white was surrounding her face, causing her to choke. She thought it was a ghost. Later she discovered that someone had hung white sheets in the loft to air. But her fear remained: thereafter, whenever she went out in the dark and if it was foggy, the muscles in her lungs went into spasm. The similarities are obvious: in both cases, it was dark and she had difficulty breathing — the first time because of the sheet she walked into and the second time because of the thick fog. With hypnosis, she learned quickly how to relax and control her asthma, as well as the itch that accompanied her eczema.

In fact, all the children with asthma that I worked with in that hospital appeared to learn how to relax very quickly. They also enjoyed the fun of seeing one little boy run up and down the corridor without a trace of a wheeze only a few minutes after he had learned how to relax himself. When I returned the following week, I was met with an hostile reception, unexpectedly so in view of the success I had achieved. I was told that the line of treatment I was using was considered to be contrary to the religious principles of those who ran the hospital.

A few weeks later, I was having coffee with the doctor in charge of the asthma ward. He said, 'By the way, I sent that little girl home as she was better.' He did not suggest that there was any connection between her recovery and what she had learned through relaxation; the fact was that instead of having to stay in hospital for the expected six months, she had returned home in a matter of a few days. Unfortunately, but predictably, the girl's parents had been told nothing of the link between her attacks, the fact that the first one had occurred in the attic among the sheets or how she could now relax easily and control her wheeze. She was thus condemned to a future of drugs when any trouble recurred. (From this, it will be seen that it is essential to involve the parents; in fact, it is often as important as seeing the child.)

Ten years later, a girl of fifteen came to see me; on taking her history, which bore no resemblance in my memory to that five-year-old child who years before had suffered from asthma and eczema, I discovered she was the very same person. Being no longer subject to the prejudices of others, she quickly relearned the relaxation techniques which had helped her previously and I gave her the cassette *Relief from Asthma* to play whenever she needed a 'boost'. During the ten years in which she had been having attacks that could so easily have been controlled, I am happy to say that there had been considerable changes in attitude towards hypnotherapy. I had even treated several patients sent to me by the religious; on one occasion, I had actually been requested by the authorities of Maynooth College (the educational centre of the Roman Catholic church in Ireland) to impart techniques of self-hypnosis to one of their priests.

One particularly pathetic case I treated many years ago was that of a young boy suffering from what is known as Harrison's sulcus. In this condition, the diaphragm (which separates the chest cavity from the abdominal cavity) goes into continuous spasm, pulling the lower ribs inward and making breathing extremely difficult. The body has a wasp-shaped appearance as a result. I had never seen anyone so deformed as this little boy. But with three months' hypnotherapy, he was able to win second place in a mountain-climbing competition. When I examined him, the Harrison's sulcus had disappeared; had he been older, this condition may have remained with him for life, but at his age the ribs are resilient and had sprung back to their normal position.

I recall another case, that of a young boy who was very ill with asthma and on cortisone treatment. He only came to see me once, since he lived over one hundred miles away, but on that occasion I taught him the principles of self-hypnosis and gave him a recorded tape to practise with. Ten years later, the boy's mother rang me, reminded me of the visit by her elder son and asked me if I would now see his younger brother, who was also suffering from asthma. We arranged an appointment and I asked her to bring her older son along as I wanted to see how he had turned out. On the day, she was accompanied by a strong, well-built six-footer, who over the years had achieved great success in athletics. I requested a record of his accomplishments and later received two pages listing his various exploits in the athletic field.

This is one of the best results I know of, but invariably every child, as far as I am aware, who has been treated with mind control for asthma has become physically above-average. There is probably no condition among children which is so easy to treat with self-hypnosis; doctors have found that most asthmatics lose their attacks almost right away, their lives transformed in the process. The successful treatment of asthmatic children is one of the most satisfying of all forms of medical practice. The children are usually keen and intelligent, although frequently anxious and sometimes extremely apprehensive. Yet it is remarkable how cheerful they are between attacks. The difference between treating such children with drugs *versus* hypnotherapy is, from the doctor's point of view, the difference between simply giving injections to stop attacks and medicines to alleviate them *versus* giving close support to the child and helping him to take away his own attacks through the harmless process of relaxation.

The training of a child in relaxation is easy, but to get the child to relax in the event of another attack is much more difficult. It is for this reason that the use of a tape recording can make all the difference. When a child, or an adult for that matter, feels himself wheezing badly, or almost choking, he may find it very hard to relax. But if a cassette is put on, one which he already knows and has come to like (one could almost use the word 'love' where asthmatic children are concerned), then it is relatively simple to relax and for the spasm to pass. Think of the difference to a child between a doctor coming and giving him an injection, and the playing of a familiar cassette, with its included suggestion that he will grow strong and healthy. To me, the efficacy of mind control over drug control is patently obvious.

While a great many sufferers from asthma get better after the first few treatments, there are those who do not and it must be remembered that the medical profession has made enormous strides in preventing and treating this complaint. But I repeat my belief that every person developing asthma has become hypersensitive to something and relaxation with a cassette should be used in almost every case.

THE ELDERLY

Elderly people can often relax very well and in the process their lives are prolonged and enriched. Many years ago, I was staying in a hotel where there was also an elderly lady and her daughter. The latter met with an underwater accident and, instead of administering the usual pain-killers, I treated her with relaxation techniques and she lost her pain. Some time later the mother sent for me during an asthma attack, but she made it clear that she would not allow herself to be hypnotised; she would only accept treatment with drugs and inhalers. I complied with her request, but she suddenly became worse and I admitted her to a private nursing home where she had a day nurse who gave her oxygen along with the usual treatment. Even though she was steadily worsening, she still refused to be shown anything to do with relaxation until, realising that her end was near, she said, 'What is the use of resisting any longer?' I asked her to relax and as she did I counted. On the count of six, six seconds later, her spasm disappeared and she went home in a few days. (The reader will be struck by the similarity of this case with that recounted on p. 45, where a medical student who had never practised hypnosis before saved the life of an asthmatic patient.)

Generally, when one sees elderly people who are very ill and who seem far from bright in their reaction, one might be inclined to feel that mind control would be ineffectual. In actual fact, these people have reached a stage of dependence and, in most cases, trust, in which it is often very easy to carry out complicated operations using a combination of simple relaxation and local anaesthetic. They respond without shock.

It is readily understandable how many elderly asthmatics respond to hypnosis, although not all respond so dramatically as the former air pilot who was referred to me by the medical officer for tuberculosis in Natal. This man told me how he was continually panting for breath and how, apparently, his condition had been caused by a number of escapades during the war. On one occasion, he had to land a plane that was in flames and on another he was brought down in the desert, where his navigator died of thirst and he just barely survived. He himself considered that these incidents were not the cause of his asthma, but that it had been brought on by flying in a plane that had no proper ventilation. He felt bitterly toward the airline responsible. Under hypnosis, however, when regressed to his first attack, a different story emerged. Regression does not always bring about a truthful answer to one's questions, but this man desperately wanted to get well and consequently he cooperated fully. He referred, under hypnosis, to his discharge from a civil airline owing to his age; following this he was spending the night in a hotel and, while carrying his bags upstairs, he had developed difficulty in breathing. Thus his first attack of asthma was associated with feelings of insecurity and uncertainty as to how to cope with his recent discharge from work, accompanied by the physical effort of carrying his bags upstairs.

There are thousands of people all over the world like this man, who are panting for breath, using bronchial dilators, taking cortisone, having injections of adrenaline and carrying inhalors with them whenever they go out. It is likely that during the time it takes to read this book, hundreds will die who could have been saved if only they had learned to use self-hypnosis to relax themselves and their bronchial muscles. Of course, some people simply cannot be treated — their chests are deformed and their tubes blocked; a small percentage just will not relax. These people need ordinary medical care but, at the same time, they can benefit from relaxation whatever the treatment they are receiving.

YOUNG ADULTS

Another group of people who are prone to asthma and other fear-induced complaints are those young adults who are experiencing 'responsibility' for the first time. Often with their feet on the first rung of the ladder, or not long married and facing all the cares of a new family, such people find themselves suddenly subject to smothering asthmatic attacks, so severe that they come to fear losing their jobs due to their frequent absences from work, thus giving rise to more insecurity and worse attacks. These young people can suffer both mental and physical torture in this vicious circle of anxiety-based illness. When they are questioned, it often emerges that in their childhood they suffered from asthma, or what they may have called bronchitis or a 'wheeze'. When they reached the age of eleven or twelve, this wheeze disappeared. This is a period of relative fearlessness, but later, as responsibilities accumulate and the once-intrepid child grows up, the physical reflex returns and causes asthma.

It is because of this dormant physical reflex that the medical profession have met with so much disappointment in trying skin tests to ascertain substances that cause allergies. Innoculating against one or more substances, we usually find that there are so many others to which the patient is allergic that this type of treatment is considered by most doctors to be a waste of time. When the same people are relaxed and allow themselves to be regressed to their first attack, it is usually found that as a child some cause for anxiety combined with certain physical conditions triggered it. One man described how, as a little boy, his mother had been ill and he worried about her. One day, while out playing in a haystack, some straw lodged in his nose and his lungs went into spasm; after that experience, they would go into spasm for other reasons. He learned to take away his attacks with hypnosis and he was, in time, freed from asthma. But if he had been happy when the straw was caught in his nose, it would not have caused asthma. It is essential, therefore, that young people learn something of mind control in order to cope with the trials of life and, when possible, to discover the cause of their first attack.

4: Weight Problems

One of the Western world's greatest health problems in this age of comparative plenty is how to prevent men and women from being, or becoming, overweight. Countless people feel exceedingly uncomfortable, no longer able to enjoy the activities they once found so pleasurable when they were slimmer and fitter. They have difficulty buying clothes which fit properly, they suffer unnecessarily from arthritis and back pains, they are unduly tired and short of breath — in short, they feel that life is passing them by.

The overweight are often caught, as it were, in a whirlpool, revolving in a vicious circle of eating followed by depression, depression followed by eating, thus compounding the problem. For those who are overweight, insurance policies are often loaded, promotion at work jeopardised and self-respect diminished. Operations, too, carry a higher mortality rate, bones are much more readily broken (even the simple 'Colles' fracture of the wrist is more common in those overweight), and circulatory and respiratory complaints are exacerbated.

Overweight has become a major problem only in comparatively recent times. For centuries, it was a dilemma facing only the rich and those few who had the opportunity of eating all they wanted. Now, however, obesity is responsible for a large proportion of the premature deaths in our society. It is interesting that in times past, when deprivation was more prevalent, a certain fleshiness was considered attractive in both men and women, and to this day there are those who suffer under the idiotic delusion that all fat babies are healthy.

Now that the numbers of those who are overweight have risen to unprecedented proportions, the methods of reducing weight, as one might expect, have become legion. It is remarkable how frequently they fail. Despite my championship of it, I am not saying that mind control will always succeed in this area. But I do believe it should always be used, either alone or in combination with some other form of treatment. Before going into the details and rationale of applying the theory of harmony between subconscious and conscious mind, thereby bringing about the discipline whereby the body achieves its normal desired weight, I will review some of the fallacies associated with the most commonly tried weight-reduction methods.

CRASH DIETS: These are usually near-starvation regimes which are supplemented, or should be, by vitamins and mineral salts. The body, in order to keep working, is forced to burn up fat. These diets have been successful with only a very small percentage of people. But even when they are effective, there are two major disadvantages: firstly, the rapid liberation of fat can flood the system with a superabundance of cholesterol, which may result in increased blockages in the arteries, and secondly, with such rapid weight reduction, the weight can return just as quickly. In the vast majority of cases it does, leaving the victims just as badly off as before, if not worse.

DIET CHARTS: These are one of the most common aids used in attempting to reduce or control weight. They usually involve cutting out the foods that weight-watchers most enjoy, with the result that when they find that they have lost weight, carelessness sets in and the forbidden foods are eaten again — first with caution, then with gusto. Usually the weight is put back on.

Apart from this fact, such diets can prove expensive and people can feel hungry while on them, so encouraging them in their half-belief that all the fuss is not really worthwhile — a notion which is perhaps the greatest disincentive to losing weight imaginable. However, there are some good diets — but, in truth, one cannot stay on them for ever.

ALL-PROTEIN DIET: A great deal of water must be taken on this kind of diet in order to flush out the waste products of the proteins eaten, which must be eliminated by the kidneys, putting undue stress on these organs. All-protein diets are also usually expensive and can only be used as a temporary measure.

SWEATING: As a means of weight reduction, sweating is effective as an expedient method of losing a few pounds quickly and is regularly used by jockeys, boxers and the like before the event. Not only is the amount of weight lost minimal, but it can only be used as a temporary measure since water is essential to life and dehydration undesirable for any length of time.

MECHANICAL MEANS: Exercise bikes, vibrators and all the other modern machines used in today's gymnasia certainly give an apparent reduction in weight. But there is no actual loss of weight. What is happening is that the muscles are being toned up, making the whole body tighter and firmer (an excellent thing in itself), so the tape measure will record a loss of inches, but the weighing scales will not register a loss of pounds.

This may seem to be a harsh review of just some of the countless methods of losing weight that have been promoted by an almost equally countless number of people. Few of us in the medical profession feel much hope when setting out to treat people who are overweight. If someone who is too fat walks into the surgery with the statement that they have fallen and hurt themselves, it is likely that they have done so because of their obesity; it is unlikely that we can prescribe anything for the condition that made them fall. We can treat the bruises or the broken bones, but few will relish treating the root cause. The problem of overweight is one which, to a large extent, has defeated us.

MIND CONTROL
This, it will scarcely surprise the reader to learn, is the method I advocate. In my experience, this approach can lead to losing weight while still enjoying what we eat. Without sacrificing anything we particularly like, weight can be reduced steadily until the exact, desired weight is reached. The one great need with this approach is consistency.

Such an ideal result may sound impossible until one grasps the basic principles underlying this line of attack. If you really wish to lose weight and let this conscious wish sink deeply into the subconscious mind, losing weight can become an easy and a pleasurable process.

The body knows when it has had sufficient food. Most of us carry on eating simply because the food is there and eating in itself is an enjoyable action. If the desire to lose weight is allowed to spread itself thoroughly from the conscious mind to the subconscious, and once the whole body has become sensitive to this mechanism, not only can overeating be stopped without undue strain but that feeling of being 'just a bit hungry' can actually become pleasant. When positive thoughts about slimming sink deeply into the subconscious, you will experience a sense of lightness and well-being, something that reminds you that you are becoming fitter because you are becoming slimmer. Positive thoughts about being slimmer are with you all day — you feel clothes becoming less restrictive, you become aware that you can now fit into smaller sizes, you find you can walk upstairs without panting. That little pang of hunger will remind you of all these feelings that you are achieving, so that you actually welcome it and look forward to the next meal.

Another interesting thing you will notice is that everything tastes so much better. You will eat your food less hurriedly and chew it more thoroughly, enjoying the various flavours you missed before, so that even if you eat less than anyone else, you do not finish first. We are always inclined to eat something we really appreciate more slowly. And at the end of the meal, you will find you are satisfied and have no desire to eat more.

Reducing weight this way does not strain the will as other dietary methods tend to do. With relaxation and mind control, the whole being is in harmony in the intention to lose weight. As you continually picture yourself becoming slimmer, more active, more fit, more attractive, your whole being rejects the idea of eating excessively — and keeps you that way.

No matter what method we use to reduce weight, it is essential to try to learn a new approach if we are going to maintain our weight at what we feel is the correct level to allow us to get the best out of life. We were all born with a great love of food, equalled only by our natural abhorrence for overeating — witness the baby who clamps his mouth shut rather than take another mouthful he does not want. It is this combination that we must regain.

The first thing to do is to find out what has gone wrong with our bodily mechanism — why we have lost those original instinctive feelings about food. Up until relatively recently, the human race had to forage for food, but the fact that we can now generally eat as much as we like, when and where we like, is not the only reason for overweight. The discovery that sugar could be extracted from cane and beet has upset one of the most important control devices in the body. Nature itself tells us when food is digestible: apples, for instance, do not taste good before they are ripe and eating them too soon can upset the stomach. When sugar is added to everything, not only do we eat food that is bad for the body but we tend to eat too much of it. (Happily, these days, many manufacturers are producing sugar-free products.)

Buried in the subconscious minds of most of us are the feelings developed in childhood. 'Eat up', 'don't waste' are instructions implanted deeply in many who have weight problems and can be an important cause of eating when they are not hungry. Many mothers, for example, will automatically eat what their children leave behind, even though they have no feeling of real hunger or desire for food. Similarly, most people dining out in a restaurant feel that leaving food on their plates, or even skipping a course, is wasteful — after all, they are paying for it. I have sounded out many people on this subject and invariably they agree that if they were out to dinner and half-way through the meal found that they were already full, they would carry on eating.

This feeling of 'don't waste' is something we can make use of because its basis lies in an essentially correct instinct. If a mother, for example, sees a piece of meat which her children have left and which she might automatically take and eat herself, she can correct this reaction by following a very simple method. She can build in the feeling of 'don't waste' by realising that since she has had as much food as her body can use for the present, then it cannot use this piece of meat. If she puts it into the refrigerator or stockpot or gives it to an animal or bird, then it is not wasted and the instinct of 'don't waste' will be appeased. If, however, she puts it in her mouth, it becomes totally destroyed and can only be carried as excess flesh, perhaps for the rest of her life. If she relaxes deeply and realises this, allowing her imagination to have full sway — picturing this feeling, so deeply embedded in the mind, of 'don't waste' — then she can view it in a different light: eating the piece of meat would be a total waste and also the potential cause of a great deal of unhappiness. This applies to any type of food — even to protein, such as meat, which contains calories that can be turned into fat.

Strong, also, in the minds of many of us is the idea that a healthy mind and a healthy body go hand in hand, so we equate a good healthy appetite with strength and fitness. Many of us have been told to 'eat up if you want to be healthy and strong' and, of course, if we did not, we could not survive. Consciously, we know that excess weight is bad for us but, unfortunately, our subconscious minds retain the notion that eating makes us strong. In fact, overeating makes us weak, flabby, prone to disease and more likely to die young. If we could unscramble these confusions and implant a natural view of eating into our subconscious minds, then the harmony between our emotions and our reasoning becomes complete.

5: Smoking

A doctor telephoned me one day to ask if I could help her to stop smoking. Her story illustrates the extreme difficulty which people experience when trying to stop smoking after being badly 'hooked'. Her specialist had told her that if she did not break from the habit, she risked sudden death. She had everything to live for and desperately wanted to stop. Dr O____, as I shall call her, described to me how she had suffered a brain haemorrhage which she was convinced had been due to her smoking. She had also had a coronary, attributable to the same cause. Neither attack nor persuasion on the part of her specialist could alter her way: she still felt compelled to continue smoking, so great was her addiction to nicotine.

This woman, with her great personal attributes and fine professional abilities, was convinced that she was unable to break from an addiction that she knew was killing her. She is representative of the many thousands of people who feel, and are, in imminent danger of death from smoking, yet who continue, admitting defeat, certain they are unable to end their dependency. Thousands upon thousands who have stopped smoking have put on weight and for this reason they start smoking again. There is also the tragic phenomenon of young people who positively dislike their first cigarette, yet who spend their money willingly and finally succeed in finding enjoyment in cigarettes. Then there are older people, suffering from the withdrawal symptoms that go with breaking a life-long habit, spending much needed money in an attempt to overcome them — and failing. Some people think that smoking is simply a matter of one's own personal choice and that too much fuss is made about it. However, the fact is that nicotine probably kills more people than any other narcotic and is probably the most addictive of all drugs.

The Irish Medical Association (IMA) called on the government in the early 1970s to implement five basic measures. They were set out in the IMA's journal and they are still relevant: to prohibit all cigarette advertising; to prohibit the sponsorship of sporting and cultural activities by the cigarette companies; to prohibit smoking in well-defined public places; to prohibit the sale of cigarettes to minors; and to ensure that laws in these areas be carried out.

If governments around the world heeded the recommendations of the medical profession in this area a great deal of suffering could be prevented and the cost of health services reduced. But the taxes received from the manufacture and sale of tobacco products usually form a significant percentage of government revenue. Yet cigarettes are a huge drain on the overall economy: people from all sectors of society drop dead in the prime of life from coronaries and, often, their dependants must be supported by the state. In a proper social society accounting, it is probable that smoking is responsible for a net loss in the resources of the nation. People do not stop spending money after they stop smoking; they simply spend the money on other things, many of which, unlike tobacco, are home-produced. Moreover, someone who does not smoke is more likely to resist being pressurised into taking other drugs, like marijuana, often supplied in the form of a cigarette. The people who supply marijuana have access to heroin and other hard drugs, a factor hardly ever taken into consideration.

A woman told me one day of how her husband had chain-smoked the same brand of cigarettes all his life and had died of lung cancer. They had nine young children and it was my view that the mother might be ethically due to compensation from the company that manufactured the cigarettes which killed her husband. More recently, such cases have actually begun to be taken to courts in Australia and the United States.

All people should consider the ethics of smoking. Is it right to kill ourselves? To leave our families bereft of financial and emotional support? Cigarette-smoking is a form of slavery. Do we like to consider ourselves slaves? Is it right to show the same apathy that was shown to the question of actual chattel-slavery at the beginning of the last century? Is it not a tragedy on a vast scale that 6,500 people die each day from smoking throughout the world, almost 2.5 million needless deaths each year?

It is 59 years since I first made a serious attempt at trying to get people to kick the smoking habit. When I was a medical student in 1930, running a summer camp for children from the slums, I set out to accomplish two things: to teach the children to wash and to show them the dangers of smoking. I do not think that anything I taught them about hygiene took permanently, but I do know that what I had to say about smoking resulted in every one of the children becoming a smoker by the end of the camp! The mistake I made was to present danger to an age group that loves danger, something which people are still mistakenly trying to do. Nor, incidentally, did I know at that time the full range of the poisons that are present in cigarettes.

Nineteen years ago I produced a record, *How to Stop Smoking.* The President of the College of Physicians in Ireland expressed pleasure at being asked to write something for the sleeve of the recording, but when he heard a sentence on the record which mentioned 'various poisons' he asked me what they were exactly. I did not know. The President said that he would very much like to use the record in his cardiac clinic, but that he could not write for the sleeve when I had stated that there were poisons in the cigarettes but did not know what the poisons were. We now know more precisely what these toxins are, especially those which cause cancer and blocked arteries. A great deal more is also known about the diseases that these poisons cause.

As I have said, it is 59 years since I first tried to get people to break from smoking. I met with failure then and it was only when I began to use hypnotherapeutic methods, combined with graphic explanations of what smoking does to the body, that I met with my first real success.

Self-hypnosis, as I continue to reiterate, is the very opposite of taking over someone else's mind. It is mind-strengthening rather than mind-bending. It is the helping of a person to reach down into their own mind to put right what is wrong. This is what makes the technique so appropriate for giving up smoking because it helps to eliminate withdrawal symptoms and replace them with a feeling of tremendous well-being, a sense of self-esteem for having kicked the habit, a greater zest for life and a more relaxed approach to it. Another of the interesting things about mind control is that if we break from a habit such as smoking, we can use the same mind control to correct other problems, such as weight control.

At first, I used a 'stop smoking' method which I now feel was a poor second-best. Essentially, this was aversion therapy: I would try to make cigarettes taste so vile that my patients could not bear to touch them, let alone put them in their mouths. What I now use is a much more effective method — to get the person to make up his own mind to become absolutely determined not to smoke; once that decision is made, I show the individual how the break can be actually pleasurable. In fact, the majority of people tell me afterwards that the feelings of release and relaxation are delightful and superior to the similar ones they used to imagine they derived from tobacco.

In order to feel this sense of release, one should know what one is being released from and in order to make this release permanent, one has to know why one is smoking in the first place. There are many reasons for this. Some start to smoke because it is forbidden: 'You are not to smoke until you are 18'. No wonder so many start — they think something great is being withheld from them. Others smoke from loneliness and boredom, or for the oral gratification it involves, or simply to be 'with it', trendy, sophisticated. This latter reason is not so prevalent nowadays, since social pressures (mainly from young people themselves) are making smoking a minority activity in many Western countries.

Most people, however, smoke because they are addicted to nicotine. This is an amazing substance, present in no other vegetation except the tobacco plant. Almost with the first puff of smoke, it is in the bloodstream. While it is a most powerful stimulant, it actually gives most people a feeling of relaxation, of satisfaction, of being able to cope. A few minutes after one cigarette, they may feel like another . . . and another. What most people do not realise is that nicotine, in common with such drugs as heroin, LSD, cocaine and alcohol, will give you a momentary lift but then dump you down with a thud, so increasing the need for another dose. The reason for this is that nicotine, amongst its many activities, attacks the nerves. It gives a feeling of uplift, but this is quickly followed by the totally opposite sensation. The person who is addicted only dwells on the feeling of well-being. The further difficulty is that nicotine is a deadly poison, one of a number of chemicals used, for example, in insecticides. One concentrated drop, if injected into a vein, would cause death. It is very hard to believe that the continual taking of this drug can actually make people feel better; many claim it does just that — they are wrong. Nicotine, like all similar drugs, acts on the nerves and leaves them very much the worse for wear. People smoke to make themselves feel better, they get worse, they smoke more . . . and so the cycle goes on.

Despite all this, nicotine is not the most lethal substance in a cigarette, although it is the one that cons most people into smoking in the first place. When we take cigarette smoke into our lungs, something else occurs. The coal tar from the cigarette attaches itself to the tiny cilia, or hairs, inside the lungs, whose function is to waft out dust or, if we have bronchitis, phelgm. When these little hairs are fouled they can, in some ways, be compared to the feathers of a sea bird fouled with oil. This is how cancer starts in the lungs. The oil in the cigarette undergoes the same change as the oil jettisoned from ships. The lumps of tar to be found on polluted beaches, which have come from the oil, have undergone that same change as have the lumps of tar stuck onto the cilia. Tar is a highly irritant substance which, when repeatedly rubbed into the skin, can cause cancer. In addition, inhaling the fumes of the heated oil from the burning tip of the cigarette causes not only cancer but also emphysema and bronchitis.

With every puff, the poisonous gas carbon monoxide gets into the bloodstream and lowers vitality. Experimental animals, with the same amount of carbon monoxide in the blood, show a marked decrease in their normal activities. As well as sapping energy, this gas also ravages the lining of the arteries, weakening them, increasing blood pressure and causing blockages in the blood vessels of the heart and legs. With Berger's disease, the legs often have to be amputated; this complaint is said to be caused by smoking alone.

I could give many more instances of the dangers of smoking. No doubt others will emerge in the future. But a few examples will suffice. If a smoker has a coronary attack, the chances of another attack are double those of a non-smoker. Carcinogens (cancer-producing substances) are circulated in the bloodstream.

The kidneys try to get rid of them and, temporarily, they are deposited in the bladder, where they can cause cancer. Cigarettes also have the effect of producing an increase of acid in the stomach which, if an ulcer is present, can prevent it from healing. The products of smoking (carcinogens and carbon monoxide, for example) reach every cell in the body via the bloodstream. The extent of the harm they do is beyond our present knowledge, but we do know a great deal about the effect of nicotine on the nerves, of coal tar on the lungs and of carbon monoxide on the heart and blood vessels. Surely these are enough to rationalise anyone's decision to stop smoking?

The various methods used to stop smoking have all done good in so far as they have helped many to break from the habit, but most have an extremely high recurrence rate. The reason for this is that, locked deep in a smoker's emotions, an equation exists linking smoking with pleasure or benefit of some sort. Most of us started smoking when quite young and those youthful feelings we had about it are inclined to persist into adult life. Even if those feelings are not conscious, they are there in the subconscious and any method which does not release us from these emotions leaves us susceptible to a recurrence of the addiction.

A study was made recently of the withdrawal symptoms of many hundreds of people who had stopped smoking by themselves, unaided. Almost every one reported feeling irritable; some even felt that they had been driven temporarily insane. In some cases, the partner of the one trying to stop had, in desperation, resorted to buying a packet of cigarettes for him or her, simply to make life less unbearable for both of them. Some reported withdrawal symptoms only readily understandable in the light of the knowledge that nicotine is probably the most addictive narcotic known to man. (A group of heroin addicts, who had tried just about everything, were asked what they considered to be the most addictive drug of all; the majority cited nicotine.)

Self-hypnosis, however, can be used to train the subconscious mind to cut off the pain of withdrawal symptoms, no matter how severe. If a person is absolutely determined to give up smoking, then he starts to give them up as an entirely positive and constructive process and the usual withdrawal symptoms can be eliminated and a feeling of well-being attained.

When people return to me who have stopped smoking but who are still suffering from withdrawal symptoms, I give them my time free of charge. I feel that very often these people have unresolved problems apart from smoking and that these problems should be tackled. I remember two cases in particular.

One involved a woman who lived with her disabled, unemployed husband and their two children. An utterly unselfish person, she had taken a man into her house who was in the last stages of terminal cancer. He was not a relative — her only responsibility to him was that he was a fellow human being who was suffering. But in doing so, she had taken on a job that was beyond the capabilities of any ordinary person. She had to look after his colostomy and feed him; five times a day she had to wash his pyjamas. She had her own children and a disabled husband to look after, and yet she had taken on this extra work purely as an act of charity. This man not only did not give her any money, he expected the children to stay quiet and objected to the dog barking.

Then one day, a few months before she came to see me, he had had to return to the cancer hospital for a check-up and from there was sent to a convalescent hospital. He cried to go back to this woman's house, but she knew she could not take him in again. She was a distressing picture when I first saw her: down to six-and-a-half stone in weight and obviously physically and emotionally drained by her attempts to help the dying man. The work she had undertaken was the equivalent of continuous nursing in a hospital, requiring the personnel of two or three shifts. Undoubtedly, she and her family would suffer greatly if she attempted to resume it. The task was obviously quite beyond her, but she still felt guilty. And as long as she felt guilty she had no peace of mind, which made her unable to cope with having broken from a habit of 60 cigarettes a day. At her weight and size, this was the equivalent of even more and she felt the withdrawal symptoms very badly. It was essential to get her to see that what she had done was almost superhuman and that to begin again to look after a man with an uncontrolled colostomy, as well as undertaking her normal domestic activities, would be quite wrong. She had to understand that her decision not to take the man back was absolutely right in every respect. She had to accept this, both emotionally and rationally, before she could regain any peace and the cessation of her withdrawal symptoms.

A second woman came to see me that same day and, like the first, she was in the grip of withdrawal problems. But she had not smoked since I had last seen her. In every other way, she was in marked contrast to the first woman. It was a strange experience seeing both almost consecutively — it had been months since any of my patients had returned. This woman was young, vivacious and had everything to live for. The story of her childhood, however, was tragic: her father had deserted the family when she was very young and her mother, not wanting her, had sent her to an orphanage, where she was extremely unhappy. Subsequently, her miserable childhood notwithstanding, she had fallen in love, married, had two children and made a happy life for herself and her family.

She spoke to me of the time when she had first married and had her own home. People would drop in during the afternoon for tea and talk — and cigarettes. Everything relating to those days was so vivid and joyous in her memory that any single thing taken from her domestic scene would upset her tremendously. The thought of never sitting down again to smoke with her friends played on her mind to such a degree that she felt severe withdrawal symptoms. All the self-hypnosis that we had used was not enough to overcome them. She had to review the situation and realise that her heavy smoking could mean the end of her happiness. Even now, after ten years of marriage, each time her husband suggested going out for a day, every second was joyous to her; when she returned home, she was filled with delight at the sight of her own front door. As she reflected, she saw how her smoking could take all this bliss away, could indeed leave her husband a widower and her children motherless. When she had meditated deeply on all this, her withdrawal symptoms disappeared. She decided to practise relaxing and, using self-hypnosis, allowed the emotions in her deeper mind to be replaced by new, forward-looking, hopeful ones. Then she left, feeling completely free.

The break from smoking can be a tremendous boost. One man who stopped sold 400% more insurance policies than he had previously done. One woman had been a journalist but, feeling that life was getting on top of her, had gradually given up work. She felt such a sense of drive and pace after the break from nicotine that she returned enthusiastically to her writing; her weight also came down along with the freedom from cigarettes.

Self-hypnosis is such an invaluable aid in giving up smoking that, once the conscious decision to stop is made, this resolve needs only to sink into the subconscious, the emotions. The withdrawal symptoms — which are the Achilles' heel of every would-be non-smoker — *can* be dealt with. As I have said, if hypnosis can cut off the severest pain, it can also be used to cut off the withdrawal symptoms from nicotine.

6: Dermatitis

The greatest enemy of the medical profession is time. Making a diagnosis of psychosomatic disorders is time-consuming; dispensing tranquillisers can be done in a matter of seconds. There is such a world shortage of doctors that there is simply not enough medical time available to give each patient sufficient to diagnose complaints involving anxiety and maladjustment, and then to treat the root causes. Every general practitioner that I know will agree with this. The answer lies in the individual learning how to face his or her own particular difficulties.

It was in 1960 that the eminent gynaecologist Mr Evans from Cardiff was invited to speak to the obstetrics branch of the Irish Medical Association about his performance under hypnosis of one in three Caesarian sections. At the end of his lecture, he said words to the effect: I never used hypnosis outside my ordinary [gynaecology] work. But one day I was asked to treat a man who had the worst skin condition I had ever seen. He was 70 years of age and had suffered from infantile eczema; his skin was now like that of an elephant. After hypnosis, it grew normally and today, it is like that of a new-born baby.

Hypnosis is one of the most effective techniques in the treatment of skin diseases. Sadly, in comparison with tranquillisers, it is seldom used. Now, skin conditions have two primary causes. The first is physical (caused by bacteria, fungi, accidents like burns, and defective circulation as in varicose veins) and should be treated by a doctor in the ordinary way. The second cause of skin disorders results from a failure in communications between the mind and the body. The skin is so readily affected by our feelings that it has been described as the mirror of the mind. People who cannot sort out their problems or see a way of dealing with them may easily suffer a rash or similar flare-up of the skin. The *psyche*, or mind, is sending wrong messages to the *soma*, or body. The ensuing conditions are then known as 'psychosomatic'.

When the human embryo is developing, the original cell divides into three different types. One of these develops into the skin, the brain and the ductless glands that produce hormones. That these tissues, which are so different, should have a common origin may be surprising, but it makes their interrelationship understandable. Thus, the close connection between the skin, brain and hormones can be seen both embryologically and psychologically. The psychological link is maintained throughout life via a two-way path between the brain and the skin. We all know how stroking and massaging the skin can waft away anxieties and make you feel calmer and happier. Think how happy a dog or a cat is when stroked. On the other hand, embarrassment can turn your skin pink, fear can make it go white and anger can make it go livid. Again, think of the dog or the cat, where the connection is so obvious — aggressiveness makes their hair stand on end. This connection between the brain and the skin is one of the factors which a sufferer from a skin condition may neglect to his peril or harness to his advantage.

A British dentist, Mr Furfil-Smith, used hypnosis extensively in his dental practice. As a hypnotherapist, he also used it to treat psoriasis (a skin disease characterised by red scaly patches). In the vast number of cases he had studied, stress proved to be the cause. His success rate in dealing with this disorder has been recorded as over 99.5% — an almost incredibly high figure, but still true. He lectured in Dublin in the early 1980s, at which time he showed photographs of the psoriasis cases he had dealt with. Sadly he has died since, but a recent documentary on British television showed him at work in his dental practice — drilling the teeth of smiling, young children whose only anaesthetic was hypnosis.

One of our most primitive instincts is to scratch our skin when it is irritated. When we are living close to nature, this might stop a flea from biting us or a tick from embedding itself in our skin; it may even help in the early stages of a fungal infection among those who do not make a religious use of soap and water. Many centuries ago, therefore, scratching was useful, since it rid the skin of actual irritants. Today, however, it is different: the instinctive reaction to scratch may be the cause of a skin condition remaining uncured or getting worse. To scratch skin suffering from eczema or psoriasis is exceedingly harmful, as it is when applied to a vast number of psychosomatic or allergic conditions.

Fortunately, it is not a case of having to choose between scratching and tranquillisers. We can use mind control. With this, the itch of a psychosomatic rash is usually alleviated within a matter of minutes, simply through practising deep relaxation. The rash itself also improves dramatically as the urge to scratch disappears. Since the human mind has a built-in ability to disregard what is unimportant and unhelpful, an understanding of the root cause of the condition can often help the sufferer to recover and to avoid the itch returning.

Among the activities of the conscious mind are those of analysis and decision-making. Orders are given through our nerves to our muscles. We do many things with our conscious minds, including thinking, speaking, hearing and moving. From our subconscious minds, orders are sent through the autonomic nervous system to all parts of the body that are outside our conscious control, including the hormone-producing glands. Almost every one of these affects the skin. These glands, unlike the salivary glands which carry saliva through little tubes into our mouths, discharge their products directly into the bloodstream. They are called ductless, or endocrine, glands. They work in harmony, under normal conditions, each affecting the other. If one over- or underproduces, a condition occurs that can be likened to an orchestra playing out of tune. When the conscious mind is unable to face or think out its difficulties and come to a rational conclusion, this leads to the subconscious mind receiving muddled information. The resultant disharmony may lead to an overproduction of adrenalin and consequently to the wrong amount of other hormones being secreted by the individual endocrine glands.

When primitive man met danger or annoyance, he would either fight or run; his adrenal glands produced adrenalin to make him better able to do either. In our 'civilised' state, if we get angry we are usually unable to either flee or fight. But the adrenalin is still produced and, because it goes unused, plays havoc with the rest of the endocrine orchestra. The effect of these glands on the skin is not only of medical interest, but is all important to those who are suffering from skin conditions. When we understand clearly how rational thinking enables the subconscious mind to give the correct stimuli to the endocrine glands, there remains only one unexplained link for us to see the relationship between an adjusted personality and an healthy and wholesome skin.

It may be surprising to most people that each member of the endocrine orchestra plays so prominent a role in controlling the condition of the skin. All the hormones seem to affect the skin in some way. Adrenalin, for example, makes the hair of animals stand erect in the presence of danger. The male hormone testosterone causes hair to grow on the face and chest; oestrogen in the female makes the skin delicate and smooth. A diminution of thyroid hormone can cause the skin to thicken, while an excess can make it smooth. Among the most remarkable of hormones is cortisone, the prized medication of the dermatologist, which, when the body is in perfect health, is manufactured in the suprarenal glands in the exact amount required.

The close connection between our state of mind and the condition of our skin is so obvious that it is essential to the effective treatment of a skin complaint that the cause should be recognised and dealt with. When a doctor sees skin disease as a symptom of a troubled mind and helps the sufferer to regain mental harmony, ensuring that no other complaint will arise to take its place, then he is fulfilling the highest purpose of medicine, as embodied in the Hippocratic Oath.

With shame and with pain, I am now going to tell you how I went through hell. A rash broke out on my wrist and then spread to one leg. Having been seen by many doctors and a skin specialist, it was diagnosed as psoriasis, but later on it turned out to be a different form of dermatitis. The rash was disfiguring in the extreme and it itched continually. It then spread to the other leg, up both sides and onto my shoulders. I wondered if I could ever be seen on a beach again and even if it would stop me practising as a surgeon. True, I had more worries than one individual should be asked to face, I thought. I was on regular emergency duty, day and night, and my wife was ill: I never knew a night's unbroken sleep. A prevailing credit-squeeze had hit me hard and, generally, my mind knew no rest. But, having been through hardships before (such as a surgical post in Liverpool during the German bombing, where I had not felt the slightest trace of nervousness), I thought I was virtually immune from psychosomatic troubles.

I decided to take some time off and went to Scotland. But still the wretched inflammation spread. Then one day I thought that possibly I was not facing up to my problems with real determination or that perhaps there was some other reason of which I was unaware. So, on this same day, I decided to listen to a cassette which I had made for others, hoping to find some truth which I had forgotten and, that by restoring my peace of mind, the skin condition would abate. My wife and I were spending the night in a guest house in a beautiful little village on the banks of Loch Lomond. On an almost deserted part of the beach, I lay in the sun and played the cassette which was aimed at helping people who could not sleep. Not that I could not sleep, but I wanted to dwell on the principles which enable the conscious and the subconscious mind to work in harmony. Soon I found the very thing that was causing my trouble: I was pushing aside difficulties as they arose, instead of facing them squarely. I decided to confront each problem as it came up, to make a definite decision as to what to do in each case, in so far as it was in my power to act — not to shelve decisions, but to take action as each difficulty arose. Further, I resolved to base my decisions on what I believed to be right, not on what was expedient.

After this, I felt a peace of mind far greater than I had experienced for a long time. The next day, the rash stopped spreading and it improved each day afterwards. The fiery red marks became duller and the scales dropped off and did not reform. Six months later all I had left were the scars, which gradually disappeared. It was a humbling experience, which I have related in the hope that it might help others.

I have since made a cassette on dermatitis, since I cannot expect others to listen to one on how to sleep better, as I did, in order to recover from a rash! If anyone thinks that all rashes should be treated individually by a doctor, without the help of a cassette, their opinion might change when they realise how many people suffer in this way. There are probably hundreds of thousands of people in the world with skin rashes that require treatment. Dealing with each one individually would be impossible, but if people knew how to treat themselves through self-hypnosis, then many people could be helped. However, it must be stressed that if a person finds his skin condition does not improve, he should consult a doctor or dermatologist at once.

Many skin diseases manifest themselves at certain ages. One of the most distressing of these is acne, which tends to affect both boys and girls as they step from childhood into the often bewildering world of adult life. This is a psychosomatic condition, brought on by the mind being thrown into confusion as it tries to adjust to new expectations and responsibilities. Very often at this age, we react in a completely different way than we have in the past, particularly in relation to our parents and perhaps also to those who have been our closest friends. With these new, seemingly insoluble problems arising, the subconscious mind receives very confused instructions. Consequently, the messages it transmits to the glands result in either an under- or oversecretion of hormones. This apparently causes the glands of the skin to become blocked and the dammed-up secretions act as a culture ground for germs — resulting in the formation of septic spots.

Acne sometimes responds quickly to relaxation techniques but, in advanced cases, the many small abscesses formed, each containing a bead of pus, may take some time to settle down. If the damage is extensive, permanent scars may be left. The ideal treatment, as in all psychosomatic conditions, should include helping the person to become adjusted. In the case of acne, however, the sufferer is usually more concerned with his or her pimply exterior than with an inner peace of mind. But even if no more than simple relaxation methods are conveyed, the benefits of these can still be great — and often dramatic.

7: Phobias

AGORAPHOBIA
The word 'agoraphobia' means either fear of open spaces or fear of crowded places; the word stems from the Greek *agora*, meaning 'a market place', and *phobos*, 'fear'. Claustrophobia, the fear of enclosed spaces, is not necessarily the opposite; in practice, the two phobias frequently go hand in hand.

It is difficult for those who have never felt intense fear of any kind to realise how housebound these sufferers are and how circumscribed and crippled their lives can become. It is surprising and distressing how little we doctors learn during our medical education of how to handle such cases. We know how to deal with a case of appendicitis or how to give antibiotics to a person who has pneumonia. But if someone comes to us who is even more ill, with fear, we can find no physical problem with them (at least in so far as we can isolate no medical cause) and so we are more or less content to say, 'there's nothing wrong that I can see.' We are not really taught how much these people need medical attention; indeed, I look back with shame on the cases I have left untreated. It is an undeniable fact that an acquaintance with the theory of relaxation therapy will help to make doctors more aware that the mind is as important as the body.

Agoraphobia shows itself in many ways; in fact, it is so prevalent I could write many pages on the subject. Suffice it to say that if you are afraid of sitting in church, of going to the cinema or supermarket, of walking down a crowded street — if such things bring on a panic attack or make you feel afraid in any way, then now is the time to act. Most of these irrational fears have a root cause which will respond to hypnotherapy.

Before the word 'agoraphobia' became fashionable, a young woman came to my surgery suffering from attacks of panic. The condition was so new to me that I did not realise how typical she was; it was only with the founding of support groups for agoraphobics that I discovered how many thousands of sufferers exist. The young woman concerned found that if her car got held up in a traffic jam, she would be so overcome with panic that she would have to abandon the car and run home. The attacks were becoming frequent and occurring under different conditions. She was newly married and although she was deeply in love with her husband she felt compelled to leave him and return to her mother. When asked if she could remember when the first attack occurred, or if there was any connection between her present attacks and some hidden fear, she could not recall anything. I asked her to sit in a comfortable chair, to allow her body to relax and then her mind. Giving the suggestion that one part of the body after another should relax, I asked her to relax more and more deeply. I then suggested that she could throw her mind back to early childhood. Nothing seemed forthcoming, however, until she was asked to wake from this sleep-like state. She then described how, one misty day when she was out with her fiancé, he wanted to go for a walk through the woods. She did not feel like going, so she sat down to wait for him. She watched him walk away through the mist. Suddenly, she panicked and fled for home. This was her first attack.

In order to help her to recall, she was once again asked to relax, one limb at a time, and to put all thoughts out of her mind except her present concern. I counted, asking her to relax more deeply with each count and, without fear, to go back year by year. I asked her to remember what exactly was brought to her mind when she wakened up, since she seemed so disinclined to speak of her childhood experiences. As she concentrated intensely, she lost her fear and the secrets of her mind, locked away by that fear, were set free.

She was brought back to her present age and awakened. She said, 'There is something I've remembered. When I was a little girl, I was told never to walk through a certain field. One day a few of us did. There was a really boggy place, a quagmire, in this field and one of us got caught in it. We pulled her out, but we dared not tell anyone about it.' The connection was now obvious. When the first attack of panic occurred in adult life, her boy friend was walking through a field like the forbidden one of her childhood; the day was as misty as it had been then. She experienced the exact same fear she had felt when her playmate sank into the mud, so she panicked and ran home. As soon as she realised the connection, she knew that this childhood experience, blotted from her conscious mind, was at the bottom of the fear that had been destroying her adult life. She also knew that, being no longer a child and understanding the cause of her agoraphobia, she need have no more fear of a misty field or of suddenly panicking for no tangible reason. Fear, in general, was now dispelled and a few weeks later her mother told me that the young woman had returned to her husband.

A case not unlike this occurred many years later. Another young woman lay in our hospital ward, terrified of having her stitches removed, her fear out of all proportion to the discomfort that she could expect to feel. Things that others could take in their stride, she would dwell on. I eventually found that there were two things she simply could not abide: one was the smell of newly cut wood, the other was the aroma of carnations. (She had even insisted that no one bring carnations to her wedding.) Both phobias were associated with the memory of her father in his coffin and the fear it had evoked. She welcomed the idea of having her stitches out under hypnosis and within a minute was so deeply relaxed that the lifting and pulling of the sutures caused no discomfort at all.

To try to get to the root of her fears I asked her, while she was under hypnosis, to throw her mind back to the time when she had seen her father in his coffin. She had been forced to look because although plainly terrified, not to do so would have been regarded as a mark of disrespect. Ever since that time, she had felt more frightened of things than she should because of not knowing the root cause of her fear. When she realised the reason for her seemingly irrational fears in general, the smell of new wood was stripped of its associations and, to my delight, she came shortly afterwards to my house and, admiring the carnations, asked me for some cuttings.

ANIMAL PHOBIAS

Millions of people the world over have irrational reactions, sometimes bordering on terror, to animals like mice, earwigs, spiders, snakes, birds, cats, dogs, cockroaches, bees, ants, 'creepie crawlies' in general, frogs — the list is long and varied. In all cases, the person feels out of control. What is the reason? In all probability, the person got a fright at an early age and this was put down to one particular thing, such as a mouse or a spider. Alternatively, a child may have seen adults terrified of something and naturally concluded that it must be dangerous. Whatever the cause, the thought is lodged deep in the subconscious.

Fear of mice is probably the most frequent cause of irrational fear. One of my patients told me she was so frightened when she went on holiday that she would spend the first half of the day looking around the room to see if there were any mice holes there. Later in life, she and her husband opened a restaurant by the sea; the setting was beautiful, she was doing the type of work she had always wanted to and business was good. Until, one day, a mouse came. The woman was struck almost dumb; she ran to her car and drove away recklessly, afraid that the mouse would climb up the wheels into the car. Then she crashed.

When she came to see me, she was terrified to return to her restaurant. Under hypnosis, I explained to her how the mouse was so helpless and harmless that it would run away from her, from anybody, rather than attack her. (It took me some time before I could reach this stage of explanation.) Then, in the mind's eye, I got her to see the mouse at a distance, so far away that she felt safe; gradually, she went nearer and nearer, still feeling safe, until the mouse ran away. Eventually she came to see the mouse as being not at all terrifying but as something really rather loving, with its young ones growing up and eating all the waste food lying around the house. Of course, I suggested that since mice multiply so quickly, we have to control their numbers. She felt safer and safer as she approached the mouse in her mind, now knowing that *it* was afraid of her.

In time, her subconscious mind, the part that deals with feelings or emotions, not thoughts, seemed to be accepting these ideas. I awakened her and sent her off with a cassette tape to reinforce the message whenever she felt she needed it. A few days later, she rang to say that she had gone back to the restaurant, looked for a mouse hole and then felt free — no longer bothered by an imaginary situation, too traumatic to analyse.

Fear of snakes is another common phobia. When I was working in Africa, we lived among snakes and many of the Europeans had a phobia about them. One woman was obsessed; in other words, she was not only afraid of snakes that were dangerous, but she was also afraid of anything that looked like a snake. Her life was a misery. She was also afraid of hypnosis and it was sometime before I could help her. When I did, her fear of snakes was brought into proportion; at the same time, she lost many other fears. She could now go for a walk, her mind free of the constant worry about snakes, and taking no more than the usual precautions to avoid them.

Back in Ireland, I treated a little boy who was terrified of snakes in the trees in case they would jump out and kill him. I told him about St Patrick killing all the snakes in Ireland and the land being free, but it made no difference. I hypnotised him and suggested to him that he was dreaming and would tell me what the dream was. He dreamt then of snakes and he saw them in the trees. I got him to realise that they were only pets and he made friends with them. This transformed his thinking and he was freed from his phobia thereafter. (It is often easy to get young children to dream and to change the dreams in a way that makes them happy.)

Other people are afraid of birds. I remember a young boy who was brought to me suffering from a very bad stammer. Neither he nor his parents had the slightest idea why it started. His parents, of course, did not know what line of treatment I would pursue. Under hypnosis, I got the boy to go back in his life to when his stammer started and he told me this interesting story. He had seen a picture, probably on the television, about birds chasing people and his fear was very real. At that time, his parents had sown a new piece of grass and he was told not to walk on it; someone told him that if he did, birds would peck him and eat him. Of course, there would have been no effect if he had not seen the picture. But with his mind filled with it, the images took over completely and he started to stammer. Once he realised that the picture was unreal and that someone had told him birds would eat him only as a precaution to prevent him from walking on the grass, his stammer disappeared.

PHYSICAL PHOBIAS

Many people are afraid of water. They cannot, or will not, learn to swim because they fear they will sink or their heads will be covered with water and they will not be able to breathe. Even heavy rain splashing over a car in which they are travelling can be sufficient to bring on a panic attack.

I remember the case of an unhappy young woman who attended one of my group sessions for giving up smoking. It is usually my practice to ask people if they have other problems, which can perhaps be dealt with at the same time. An interesting thing happened with this young woman: under hypnosis, she told how as a young girl she had been pushed into a lake by her brothers. Although she was a good swimmer, she had got a bad fright and the terror of seeing the water coming up into her face remained with her to this day in her subconscious. Life became sour after that incident; she had no real friends and did not know why she was so unhappy. Now the significance of the event became clear to her: she saw that she had been pushed in for fun and for no more sinister reason. (This is a typical case — often misunderstanding of an action can cause immense fear in later life.) Quite unexpectedly, she had freed herself of her deep-rooted fear and she returned the following week, radiantly happy and at peace with herself.

Fear of thunder is experienced by many people. They go to pieces when they hear the loud claps or the menancing rumble above them. It is essential that such people accept the positive fact that thunder is harmless and of no danger to them (the lightning that precedes the thunder can, of course, be dangerous). In the rare cases where something is hit and has fallen down, by the time the sound of the thunder reaches us from out in the atmosphere, we know that we are safe — this is what makes fear of thunder so irrational.

Mrs G____ was a woman obsessed by thunder. If she heard on the radio that the day was going to be cloudy with rain, she would become almost hysterical. Yet, she had no fear of dying or of being injured. As a rule, such a fear can come from a physical cause, but more likely it derives from other people who were terrified in their minds of thunder. Mrs G____ felt that the latter was true in her case and she told a most interesting story. When she was a little girl and there was any thunder, even far off in the distance, her mother would be terrified and bundle all the children into bed with her. She would pull the covers up over them and wait for the 'storm' to pass. As a child, Mrs G____ had felt that there really was danger, that the house might fall down and they would all be killed — all this set off by her mother's reaction.

When I hypnotised her, I wanted to replace the erroneous thoughts about thunder she had from her childhood. I suggested that she heard a sound and it would make her more relaxed. (I clapped my hands to make a sound.) I gradually increased the loudness of the sounds until the banging of metal simply made her more relaxed still. I described to her how as a small child under the blankets she had heard sounds like this. But she had misinterpreted them. Now she could picture herself growing up, unafraid of thunder or anything else. Years later, a man came to my surgery; he had been recommended by Mrs G____ and he reported that she was entirely free of her phobia.

There are many stories like this. In all cases, the same thing emerges — how the original problem has to be found and faced, then looked upon in a different light and using the principles of self-hypnosis for relaxation, the mind freed for good.

Fear of flying is becoming more and more common these days. Of course, in our increasingly busy world, where safety and economy sometimes do not seem compatible, there are real fears and the number of aircrashes in recent years does little to reassure the public. But there are also thousands of people who have a totally irrational fear of flying — some are afraid of enclosed spaces, some of dying, some do not trust the pilot or the plane, others simply do not know what it is that terrifies them. How can they get over this fear? It is essential that they have the following facts in their conscious minds and through relaxation allow them to reach the subconscious: planes are safe, one of the safest ways of travelling, and it is right that we go by plane; planes are serviced and inspected in a way that cars, our ordinary means of transport, never are; pilots have to undergo stringent medical tests at regular intervals; in addition to the pilot, there is a backup system (the automatic pilot) on most larger planes; and finally, but most importantly, the crew and staff all want to get back home too.

By relaxing deeply, you can allow such positive thoughts about flying to enter the subconscious mind. You can face the problem of how your fear of flying started in the first place; then picture yourself feeling the fear going away, as you relax with your present knowledge that it is safe. This may seem simplistic, but perhaps when you have relaxed deeply enough, you will feel it well within the human capacity to accept new ideas of freedom and happiness.

When the time for the flight comes, you can occupy yourself in various ways, by, for example, finishing an exciting novel that you have kept specially for this occasion.

I have dealt successfully with many people who feared flying. One man not only got over his fear of being flown — he took up flying himself and operates his own plane commercially. Another, a businessman, was terrified of flying to North America; having dispelled his fear, he enjoyed his flight so much that he bought an inter-city flight ticket to travel from place to place, thus saving himself time and money.

Dentistry is another area where hypnotherapy can be of tremendous value. Many people are afraid of having their teeth filled, yet when we consider the care that dentists take of their patients, it is obvious that this is an irrational fear, most likely brought on by some earlier traumatic event. We are given one set of teeth in our lifetime and these should last us if only we would refrain from eating foods which enable bacteria to grow and cause tooth decay; those of us with false teeth would give anything to have a full set of normal teeth again. Nowadays, the emphasis is on prevention of decay, by dental hygiene, and in any dentist's surgery we will find a booklet which tells us how we can grow up and have good healthy teeth, even in old age. Let us grasp this opportunity — or at least allow our children to grow up free from decay. But if we need our teeth filled, we can learn how to have this done in comfort, by relaxing so we feel no pain at all during the short time needed to drill the hole. Children are particularly good subjects for this and it is an area well worth developing for later life.

I remember, many years ago, an old graveyard was dug up beside my home, part of which dates back 800 years. The graveyard was even older. The soil was dumped in my garden and in it I found a great number of skulls, all small although they belonged to adults, indicating that the people of Ireland at that time were of a much smaller build than today. Most of the skulls were intact and contained a full complement of teeth. These were flat, like the teeth of a horse, apparently from eating grain. Only in one case did I find a cavity in a tooth. Obviously, before sugarcane was discovered and added to all our foods, teeth lasted a lifetime for these people.

8: Learning Problems and Passing Exams

Before I was a medical student, I would have given a great deal to have been able to learn with the facility of some others. But, one day, notwithstanding, I decided to undertake the seemingly impossible study of medicine. It was then that a complete change in my outlook took place. Every subject was suddenly full of importance and the specifically medical studies became of the most intense interest.

In the event, I was extremely fortunate in that I was introduced to a man who gave a 'grind' in chemistry and it was under his tuition that I learned the technique of building knowledge upon the foundations of existing knowledge. This man's excellent principles of learning have stayed with me ever since. Their efficacy lies in their simplicity — and I do not hesitate on that account to give a description of them.

With him, each day, I learned something new, but I also went back over what I had already covered, so that every single thing I was taught I retained easily and each new fact built upon the knowledge that I already had. My tutor lived in a small house in a poor part of the city; he possessed no formal qualifications and had blown two fingers off one of his hands while experimenting in chemistry — a subject about which his knowledge was quite extraordinary. He captivated me entirely. Before going to him, the subject seemed too impossibly vast for me ever to be able to master. I began with no knowledge of chemistry whatsoever and only six weeks in which to prepare for the exam. He covered the entire course in four weeks, by concentrating on the essentials and by making sure that what I did learn, I learned and understood perfectly. In the fifth week, by way of revision, he covered the entire course again, and in the sixth week, once more.

When the time came for the examination, I found an amazing thing happening — the examiners seemed to think in exactly the same way as my tutor. For the first time in an exam, I found that instead of having a vague knowledge of rather a lot, I knew the essentials in great detail. When the time came for the oral part of the exam, to my surprise and delight, every question that I was asked I had twice covered and revised. I saw the examiner write down '100%'.

Through this tutor, my despondency had evaporated and I had come to love the subject and, naturally, be more competent in it. Even now, 60 years later, I can remember things he told me as if it were this morning. Of even greater importance was the fact that the basic principle of learning which he had instilled in me helped with the next subject I had to tackle, and the next … Every lecture became of interest and every exam fun.

When the mind is wholly on its work and not overtired, knowledge is gained out of all proportion to the times when we study with only half a mind on the subject. Sometimes we think that we can study just as well, and much more happily, with the radio or record-player going. If the theory is tested, however, we would find that what has been learned with the music playing is only a fraction of that taken in without these distractions and with the mind entirely concentrated. We sometimes study when we are tired, believing that we are getting through a great deal of work, when, in fact, probably very little is sinking in. When tired, we should stop and rest, and resume studying when the mind and body are refreshed. Then what is learned is much more easily retained and readily recalled.

As a boy, I remember reading an article on proportional representation and being completely absorbed by it. From that day, I have never had any difficulty in understanding the question fully. But when something I read holds no interest for me, or when I am tired and my mind is unable to concentrate fully, I forget what I have read almost immediately.

This is a vital point and worthy of consideration. If we think of all the facts learned at school, and the number retained only a few years afterwards, it is obvious that the majority were learned in vain. One of the few dates most people remember from schooldays is 1066; it would have been better to have a dozen dates indelibly printed in our minds than to have been given hundreds, most of them quickly forgotten. If we know that 1066 was the Battle of Hastings, for example, and then were told about something which happened five years later, it would be related back to that battle, thereby standing a much better chance of being remembered. A date in a 'vacuum' is rapidly forgotten by most people, but when we learn a fact that can be related to one we already know, then it is more likely to be retained. If we make certain that the facts we do learn are fully understood, gone over time and time again, they become a part of us and are easily recalled whenever required, even under the pressure of an exam.

To prevent ourselves forgetting something we have learned, a short note of it and frequent glances at the note is a good way of revising. I remember as a student going up for one of the most difficult exams I ever had to take, one that only qualified doctors are now allowed to take. The night before, I read over the short notes that I had made and in so doing read the answers to all the questions. One hour, and these brief notes, made the exam quite easy.

I was staying at a hotel once where I met a headmaster, who was accompanied by his twelve-year old son who could not spell. The boy, like everyone who has difficulty in spelling, hated the subject. He would look at the words he had been given to learn, feel hopeless and wish he could be anywhere else in the world. In this frame of mind, the ability to learn is at its lowest ebb. His whole attitude needed to be reversed. Once he gained confidence, he could see the fun of being able to spell and read rapidly, and also the advantage of having more time for extra-scholastic enjoyments. One of the first steps in bringing about this confidence was to take a simple word that he could spell easily and then ask him to spell it backwards. At first, he was unable to do so. I wrote the word down and he studied it, then I covered it with my hand. After a few moments, he was able to picture the word, even when it was covered, and spell it backwards. He then found he could take a more difficult word and learn to spell it rapidly in the normal way because, for the first time, he was seeing each letter clearly. Hypnosis was used to help him accept facts more quickly and, although it was not essential, it helped him to concentrate, absorb the knowledge and adjust more readily. At the end of the week, he told me that he had come first in spelling at school. I told his father, who simply would not believe it. His son had done no work, he said. So I asked him to inquire at the school and the next day he told me that it was true, but added, 'I had given him a good telling off for not spelling properly!' He believed that his lecture had worked! His attitude typifies that of so many who stand unthinkingly in the way of progress, being one of those who are unconvinced, who see but do not comprehend, and so stifle one of the most useful techniques available to us — hypnosis.

A woman told me once that her husband could not write, but impressed upon me the fact that I must never let him know that she had told me. She explained how he had built up a large and successful business and how, at the end of the week, he would go to the bank and collect the salaries of his employees in cash, since he was incapable of writing out a cheque. I told her of the difficulties I had had in learning how to spell and that I felt I could talk to him tactfully. When he came to my consulting room and realised that I had felt some of the agony he suffered and that I was not in any way talking down to him, he felt less uneasy and was willing to try and learn. To his wife's surprise, he knew all the letters of the alphabet, but was unable to read even a two-letter word. Obviously, he had some extreme mental block. The thought of school and learning conjured up such fear and shame in him that it was as though his mind had closed down completely on the subject of reading. I wrote down in block letters the word 'it' and asked him to spell it backwards, which, of course, presented no problem to him. I then covered it with my hand, as I had done with the headmaster's son, and he was still able to spell 't i' without difficulty. I then told him that 'i t' spelled 'it' and that I was going to cover the word again, but this time I wanted him to spell 'it' forwards. His reaction was as if something had hit him — as if he were being asked to do something of which he was totally incapable. When he realised that it was no more difficult to spell 'it' forwards than backwards, he no longer associated spelling with being trapped and terrified at school. Instead, he was doing something that was well within his reach. He went on from word to word, spelling them as if he were playing a game, first backwards and then forwards. Eventually, he was able to write down his own name. When he wrote his wife's name, she was thrilled. Three weeks later, she told me that her husband was now writing out the pay cheques.

So many people who are totally illiterate find such devious ways of hiding their disability that the extent of their problem is not easily recognised. We can readily grasp the enormity of a person's dilemma who cannot read the destination of a bus, a street name, a warning sign or the day of the week from a newspaper.

A man came to see me for help in order to stop biting his nails. He learned rapidly how to relax and to picture his nails growing normally, learning to detest anything that would spoil their appearance, and so they quickly grew. It was only after this that he was able to talk about his main problem, which was his inability to improve himself at work. He went to night classes, but found it impossible to study. He would try to listen to a lecture but, as one sentence was being spoken, his mind would still be on the one before, so missing the whole train of thought. He was married with a young family and anxious but unable to improve his education, which was necessary for his advancement at work. He had received the normal schooling, but had been a poor scholar. There was obviously a mental block present, as there possibly is with every otherwise normal person who has difficulty learning.

But what block? That was the question. He had already proved that he could cooperate in relaxation — his nails were now perfect. So I decided to use a technique I had learned in hospital in Pretoria. I asked him to sit in a chair and allow his whole body to relax. He was to think of first one arm relaxing and then the other, and so on, right round his body. He was asked to put all thoughts out of his mind as far as he possibly could, except those of relaxing and becoming drowsy — I told him that, as I counted, his eyes would become heavy and he was to allow them to shut as soon as they did so. Soon his eyes closed and he drifted into a concentrated state of relaxation. I asked him to picture himself walking into a theatre, up towards the stage and then sitting in the front row; he was to lift his index finger when he felt himself sitting down. He did this after a few minutes. On the stage there was a man whom I described as having the same features as my patient. I explained how this man on the stage found himself unable to improve his position at work because he was unable to learn properly but that, on the stage, behind a screen, lay a solution to his problem.

I then asked my patient to think of himself as one year younger, going back from the age of 35 to 34, and then further back, until he reached early childhood. At this point he became exceedingly agitated. I felt just as apprehensive myself, certainly just as excited. I told him that he need not worry, that he would remember everything he saw when he returned to his present age. I counted the years back up to 35, then asked him to wake up and tell me what was behind the screen. Behind it, he said finally, he saw his mother and father fighting and that he simply could not listen to what they were saying to each other. He told me how his parents had fought continuously and how he would hide the carving knife in case his mother might kill his father; then how, when he was nine, his father abandoned the family and this had dogged him all through his schooldays, even up to the present. What affected his study now was an inability to listen attentively — an extension and perversion of the deafness he had inflicted upon himself in order to shut out his parents' quarrelling. When he realised these things and how, now, as an adult they no longer needed to affect him, he became a different person. I met him about a fortnight later. He said he had been to a lecture on *King Lear*. I quizzed him about the play and the names of some of its characters; I could not fault him on anything — he could even reel off the names of the King's legitimate sons and those that were bastards! This was an exceptional case and not many of us will attain such brilliance.

Apart from the abilities we are born with, to learn anything we need enthusiasm and a willingness to work. But we also must have a sense of fun, adventure and abandonment. There are probably countless people like myself who, as children, found it difficult to learn another language. Even after years of study, I still felt incapable of putting even a few sentences together and I was unable to pronounce any word that contained one of what seemed to me, strange, throaty, guttural sounds. Shortly after qualifying in medicine, I was offered a locum in central Africa, where I joined with the locals in singing at the top of my voice in their language, with all its guttural sounds. Now, without any inhibitions, I found that I could not only pronounce but sing words which I had found absolutely impossible before. If I had felt this same abandon at school, I am convinced I could have learned French, Chinese or any other language.

When my six months' locum was up, I travelled to South Africa and there I found, what were to me, the most extraordinary sounds being made and used as parts of words. For example, a drawing-away of the tongue from the palate made a sound like that of a cork being pulled from a champagne bottle. The name of one tribe begins with this exotic sound, sometimes called the 'click' and usually rendered in print as 'X', followed by 'osa'. One day I met the headmaster of a school in the Xosa area and, in conversation, I happened to mention the name of the tribe. He looked at me in amazement — he had lived in that area for over 30 years and still could not pronounce it.

I could hardly recognise myself, released as I was from this mental block. Now, so many years later, I have neither the time nor the opportunity to learn a new language, which I feel I could so easily have done in my younger days had I been helped and freed from this block. I am on holiday in Portugal as I write this chapter and, having arrived a few days ago, I have succeeded in obtaining a phrase book. Now I find myself using Portuguese to buy things, coming back with the right articles and, what is more, the right change. At an age when it is difficult to learn a language, I find that I have learned more in a few hours than I did in months at school — simply out of pure abandon, not minding making mistakes, listening to corrections with interest and finding everything fun. I noticed the similarity between the words I knew and those I did not and, putting difficult words on a tape, kept repeating them until I could say them. Then I went out of my way to use them with the Portuguese.

I would like to say a few words in passing on the subject of 'sleep learning'. I believe that no one learns *in* their sleep — I have reached this conclusion after contacting and investigating centres where this supposed technique is taught.

If we are in a deeply relaxed frame of mind, with concentration at its maximum and with an absence of effort, the brain absorbs at its fastest — just as a child will learn a new language seemingly without trying. It is common knowledge that when we are on the verge of sleep, our minds are at their most receptive. If we need to get up in the morning at a particular time and we go to sleep with that idea firmly planted in the mind, then it is almost certain we will wake at the time desired, however early. The same applies to any other thoughts that are allowed to sink into the mind as we are drifting off to sleep. This period can be used by a parent to reassure an asthmatic child. In China, parents use this time to implant confidence in children who wet their beds and this has proved effective.

The first lessons from one organisation promoting sleep-learning were, in fact, hypnotic techniques and, only after these did the tapes mention language-learning. One ingenious method of using the period between going to bed and falling asleep, and that between waking and getting up, was the use of an apparatus that played the tapes for a set period of time and then switched off, coming on again half an hour before the time for getting up. I believe that we can certainly utilise this period of heightened receptivity for rapid learning, but I am convinced that no learning takes place while we are actually asleep.

I will close this chapter with an account of a man we will call 'Seamus', which I referred to earlier when dealing with stage hypnosis (see p. 16). At the time, our hospital had been moved to new premises, where my consulting room was so big that it was later to be used for meetings and physiotherapy sessions. One day, in the middle of my out-patients' surgery, two men excitedly dragged in a third, who was semi-conscious. They dumped him on my couch, where he immediately went into a deep hypnotic trance. This happened 28 years ago, when I had been working with the subconscious mind for only a few years. Never before had I seen such a case.

It transpired that he had been hypnotised many times on stage and, had he been left alone, would have drifted into a normal sleep from which he would have been wakened when rested, or from which he could easily have been roused, if he were following the normal pattern of a person who had been put into a trance and left. But here, I had a waiting room full of surgical patients, all of whom had been referred by their doctors, and on my couch was a man in a deep hypnotic trance, who subconsciously believed himself to be under the control of a stage hypnotist. I had been to this man's shows and understood what had happened. The entertainer stated that he did not use hypnosis, but thought transference through a sixth sense. Seamus had apparently been left with the post-hypnotic suggestion that he would   go into a trance on hearing a certain word.   At work, one of his mates had mentioned the word for a joke, not realising the danger.

I knew that if I used the methods of the entertainer and roused him from his trance, he would immediately see that I was not the man he believed was controlling his thoughts and would be likely to fall back into the trance. Instead, I deepened it and brought him under my control. Then I told him I would count backwards from 30 and that as I did so he would gradually wake up. During this time, I also told him that he had been under the influence of the entertainer, but that now he was released from that influence. I added that he would not be under my influence or that of anyone else who might try to control his subconscious mind, unless he wished to be. As the countdown came to an end, he was already waking up and on the sound of 'one' was completely alert and able to return to his job.

The sequel came when Seamus was admitted to our surgical ward following a motor-cycle crash. He told me that he had been to the hypnotist's show again, but that he no longer felt drawn to the stage. His immediate problem was blood inside his knee joint which had to be drawn off. Since he was such a good hypnotic subject, it took less time to induce numbness in his knee by hypnosis than it would to fill a syringe with a local anaesthetic — and much more pleasant. The blood was removed without any sensation at all.

What followed is, to my mind, of profound importance, since it gives an insight into the workings of the mind of a frightened child when he first goes to school, which fear, if it goes unrecognised, may turn a brilliant child into an intellectually underdeveloped adult, maybe even an illiterate.

Seamus was of a nervous disposition and, while drawing the blood off his knee, I asked him to throw his mind back to his early childhood, to the time when he first felt really afraid. He regressed in time to his experience of school. He was terrified. Everything was indelibly imprinted on his mind, as the past is imprinted on all our minds, buried for the most part in the subconscious. Yet it is often these buried memories that play the most important parts in our lives. When taken back in time, he relived every second of it. He told how his father fetched the pony and trap, ready to drive him to school, and how, in his terror, he hoped against hope that something would go wrong with the trap so that they would have to turn back. But nothing did go wrong and he arrived at school, his terror increased. Every detail was vivid in his mind, from the exact item and colour of clothing that his teacher wore, down to the position of each pupil in the class. Every movement his teacher made filled him with apprehension and when she wrote something on the board he was certain dreadful things would result. Then she came towards him — and handed him a sixpenny piece. This was something unexpected. His fears vanished: she might be kind after all. His fears returned slightly when she started to teach the class again. But the gesture of the sixpenny piece could never be removed from his emotions and his subconscious mind.

I took a recording of all that he had said, the second-by-second account of his first day at school. And what he said showed not only what fantastic potential he had for learning and recall, but how easily a child's mind can receive a mental block through fear. For had there been no kindness shown, fear could have prevented him from learning — so important is the environment to doing so and so conducive is the human mind.

9: Alcoholism

Many grieve at the suffering in the world, yet their expenditure on alcohol far outstrips the few coins they may drop into the collection box on the bar. Many people find that alcohol is spoiling the fun of living — for themselves and for those around them. They may sincerely believe that they are not alcoholics and convince themselves that there is nothing really wrong. Yet I have known the money such people have blithely spent on alcohol to be as much as the cost, for example, of a yacht on which the whole family could enjoy themselves.

I once made a tape for patients who were alcoholics. Shortly after, I received a visit from a representative of the Department of Health, which works with alcoholics, who asked me if I would produce this tape for general use by the public. When I said that I felt it was not nearly good enough, he asked if I would like some help. This resulted in the most enlightening meetings taking place every week in my home. I live in an old Norman castle and there, in front of a log fire, gathered alcoholics under treatment, former alcoholics with their wives and children, and social workers who told me what they had learned from their experiences with alcoholism.

The former alcoholics, especially those who belonged to Alcoholics Anonymous (and many of whom would dispute that there is such a thing as a 'former' alcoholic — they maintained there are alcoholics who are drinking and there are alcoholics who are sober, but they are all alcoholics), enlightened me about the reasons why they felt misunderstood, not only by their families and friends but, more especially, by the medical profession. They all listened to the tape I had made and then, metaphorically, tore it to shreds. I remade it and we met again the following week. But, still, it was far from right. One after another told me how, at a certain point, they would have turned the tape off. It was then, and only then, that I realised I had to learn a new language in order to communicate with alcoholics. One person thought that they were wasting their time in trying to get doctors like me to understand their problems. But when he saw that my aim was to learn in order to help, his opposition turned to enthusiasm.

Before these workshops took place, I had said something which I now recall with shame and incredulity at my immaturity. To those of you who are not alcoholics, I wonder how quickly you can spot the three gross mistakes in the following sentence: 'Those of you who are alcoholics must realise that you cannot go out with the intention of taking only a few drinks.' Please spend a few moments trying to find the faults.

They are: (1) an alcoholic does not go out with the idea of having a few drinks, but of having one and being able to stop; (2) he or she is allergic to the word 'must'; and (3) 'Those of you who are alcoholics . . .' I was speaking from a pedestal, where I was different; I had to explain my way back into the friendship of those who felt I could never understand, by saying that, although I was not an alcoholic, I had other sins, flaws and imperfections, and was therefore no better than those who were excessive drinkers.

When I reworded the sentence to, 'Those of us who are alcoholics would do well to remember that we can never go out with the idea of having only one drink,' then it became acceptable. But the tape I produced the following week was again torn to pieces by the former alcoholics, who insisted that alcoholism was a disease. One man, who had given his life to the treatment of alcoholism and risen from being a complete down-and-out to becoming a successful author, wrote me six pages proving, as far as it was humanly possible, that alcoholism was a disease. An addiction is, of course, a very understandable disease and I finally accepted that there is a basic truth in this, although the disease is very different from those caused by tumors and micro-organisms. Week after week my tape was faulted until, finally, all were satisfied with its contents, even to the extent of saying that had they listened to it earlier in their lives, they felt they might have been spared years of hell.

One of the group insisted that the production was not good enough. He explained that he had worked professionally in a recording studio and offered, if I would do the same, to give up some of his time in order to produce a polished tape. This was done and it was then, more than ever, that I realised how much truth there was in what alcoholics had so forcibly expressed — that every alcoholic is basically a perfectionist. At first, this fact seems unrealistic and unacceptable — so many lives lived in squalor, with families feeling that life is hell — until one realises what perfectionism does to people (see p. 106).

The alcoholics said they especially liked one part of the tape, where they relaxed and imagined themselves drinking, tasting their favourite tipple and feeling all those sensations of release, entering, as it were, another world, a world of happiness, and then returning home with the money still in their pockets and with the feeling of remorse replaced by one of freedom and tranquillity. This turned out to be the most important part of the cassette, for the greatest thing that alcoholics wish to achieve is a feeling of contentment that is not gained through drinking.

There were certain points on which every alcoholic present agreed: they were emphatic that alcoholism is a disease, that almost every alcoholic is a perfectionist, that someone who has been an alcoholic remains an alcoholic for life, however many years he or she has been sober, and that the break from alcohol must be complete.

Most of the cassette for alcoholics is concerned with how to find freedom from alcohol and how the use of self-hypnosis can be of such enormous help in this search. When the tape was produced, I gave one to a publican who had been admitted to my ward with abdominal pain. I asked him if he would listen to it and tell me what he thought. When he gave me his opinion I was more than surprised, since I had no idea that he himself was an alcoholic. He would never drink in his own pub, he told me, but once it was closed, he would go to a nearby hotel where he would drink heavily every night. Later, after using the tape, he decided to sell his pub and open a restaurant. Incidentally, his abdominal pain ceased when he stopped drinking — it had been due entirely to his excessive alcohol consumption.

Stranger still, to me, was an incident which began when a man was brought into hospital with a dislocated elbow. The beginning of the story is quite intriguing and the end, really rather funny. It happened like this. I had a group of smokers in my surgery and an RTE presenter, who had come as an observer because of an interest in alternative medicine. I was interrupted in the middle of the session and told that a man with a dislocated elbow was in the out-patients' department of the hospital. I made my apologies and, taking the presenter with me, drove the half mile to the hospital. Once there, I inspected the man's X-rays, hypnotised him, reset the dislocation, immobilised the arm in a splint and told him what exercises he should do before I saw him again next week. I was back in my surgery with the smokers within sixteen minutes. I only mention this to point out that, without rushing, the whole procedure had taken less than twenty minutes, the alternative in those days being to admit the man to hospital, administer a general anaesthetic after a certain period of time and then retain him for a number of hours afterward, all this involving the valuable time of several medical staff.

The upshot of this case was that when the man returned the following week for a check-up his elbow had mended well, but he was anxious to know if I could help him with another problem he had had for some time — a hiatus hernia. (This condition occurs when the opening in the diaphragm through which the oesophagus passes becomes enlarged and muscular contractions, passing in the wrong direction, carry acid with them from the stomach, causing a burning sensation in the lower gullet. Tension is frequently present and is possibly the cause.) The man admitted he was tense and wished to overcome his tension. But because I was incredibly busy at that time, I was only able to give him a recording I had made for my insomniac patients on *How to Sleep Better*. This would demonstrate to him many of the principles whereby one can obtain harmony of mind and freedom from anxiety.

The man returned the following week. I asked him, 'How did you get on with the record?' 'All right', he replied. That was all — he said no more. Using the same tone of voice, I asked, 'What do you mean by "all right"?' 'I don't know what drink has got to do with my hiatus hernia!' came the hurt reply. It turned out that the record manufacturers had put the wrong label on the record. The interesting thing that came to light then, after we had sorted out the mistake, was that the man had dislocated his elbow when he had fallen off a chair owing to his heavy drinking. He was, in fact, an alcoholic. He went on to say that he had not touched a drop since playing the tape. This was most gratifying to me.

While self-hypnosis can be of tremendous help in alcoholism, in eliminating the withdrawal symptoms and giving a new perspective, it is usually necessary for a person to go to Alcoholics Anonymous (or any of the other organisations) who will help in many ways; they will, for example, ring up a man before he gets his paypacket and meet him to accompany him home. This is but one of the dozens of helpful things recovered alcoholics will do for each other.

Perhaps of equal, or even greater importance, is the effect of alcoholism on the relations of an alcoholic: the number of people affected and the trauma caused to members of the family is inestimable. The late Erskine Childers, while Minister for Health, estimated that five relatives are admitted to mental institutions in Ireland for every one alcoholic admitted. To the relatives and children of an alcoholic, the organisations of AA, Al-Anon and Al-Ateen can be of enormous benefit, both to themselves and in learning how to understand, communicate with and help the alcoholic overcome his problem.

10: Perfectionism

I remember a certain lady telling me that her life was full of stress. She could never be satisfied with what she had done, because she had so little time and was always tired. She would dust and vacuum-clean the rooms with her family sitting around. When asked if she ever played with her children she said, 'No, I haven't time.' I asked her if her family appreciated the place being so clean and tidy and she said they didn't care at all.

It was evident to me that this woman was a perfectionist. She could not sit in front of the fire if the hearth rug was in the least bit crooked. She was forever trying to make things more perfect. Her family were fed up with her constant fussiness. I could see no hope for the poor woman unless she could learn to be content to enjoy life as it must be lived in this imperfect world, with things as good as they need to be.

Why is it that if you were to ask a group of people under treatment for alcoholism, 'Are you perfectionists?', you are likely to be told, 'Of course, don't you know we all are'. Perfectionism is one of the things that has driven them to alcohol. If we were to find out the number of people who enter mental hospitals because of perfectionism, we would realise the damage that it is doing to our society.

The greatest man that ever lived said, 'Be ye perfect as your Heavenly Father is perfect'. And to hundreds of millions, these words are axiomatic. Why then do I say that perfectionism is harmful? It is because perfectionism is the enemy of perfection. It is hoped that an examination of why this is so may help to dispel a misunderstanding which has caused much misery and a tragic lack of fulfilment in so many lives.

The question mark stands out in bold relief: why does perfectionism lead a man to have one foot in the gutter, a house containing nothing but empty bottles and an unhappy family? Why, too, is the perfectionist constantly at risk from depression? The answer is that perfectionism has its origins in pride. This does not mean that all perfectionism is harmful or bad. It is essential to distinguish between that 'being perfect' which is constructive and gives fulfilment and that which causes such enormous ravages. An attempt to do a thing perfectly is excellent if we have a deadline on our time; if we do not it is devastating. I personally have felt the greatest satisfaction and fulfilment when working with lacerated faces, using plastic surgery techniques and not allowing time to matter (within the limits of the procedure not being too time-consuming or traumatic for the patient). I felt happy when I saw that the scars were minimal and once, delighted when I reviewed three cases in succession where no scars could be found. This is perfectionism at its happiest.

Where perfectionism kills and destroys, however, is when we are discontented unless something is unnecessarily perfect. Take the simplest of situations: many a mother's heart is full of sorrow because she has not heard from her son who has gone abroad to work. Even half a page would fill the void. The son, who does not understand perfectionism, feels differently; he thinks that a few lines aren't good enough and that he must get down one of these days to writing a decent letter. More sorrow is the result. Again, an artist may begin a beautiful painting but, because it never reaches his highest expectations, it remains unfinished, confined to oblivion. It has been said of William Butler Yeats, among the world's greatest poets, that he was inclined to reword and revise his poems to such an extent that some of them were simply refined out of existence, lost forever.

Sometimes perfectionism takes a strange course — a person dislikes his own handwriting and so uses a typewriter. Finding one day that he is without one, his dislike of his own handwriting results in his simply not writing anything. But much worse than this, a person may feel satisfied only if he is on top; being second-in-command won't do. Perfectionism can divide and destroy a home. Perfectionists look for perfection in their spouse and children, with the result that the spouse may have a nervous breakdown or the children become seriously disturbed. As in the case that introduced this chapter, perfectionism in a mother can prevent a house from being a home and drive her children away.

We can gear our desire for perfection to making other people happy. We can achieve this by simply doing our best *in a given period of time*. We can learn to live with things which are imperfect. We can have time to spare for the things which really matter. You may feel that all this is good advice for people who are perfectionists. But there are various degrees of perfectionism and many of us are caught in one or another aspect. Some of us, for example, cannot speak in public. You may ask what has that to do with perfectionism? If we did not think of ourselves as being important, only of what we have to say as being worthwhile, then we would be free of our self-consciousness. This is a vital point in getting rid of stammering or blushing, too.

11: Insomnia

Countless millions go to bed every night, hoping they will sleep. But sleep eludes them. During the day, they feel tired and often fall asleep while reading or watching television — in other words, when they are relaxed. But when they go to bed, they cannot sleep. They suffer from insomnia, one of the complaints that receives less attention than the rarer diseases.

Normally when we go to sleep, we drop into a state of relaxation in which ordinary sounds do not disturb us and the little aches and pains we usually suffer disappear. We dream and forget the dreams afterwards. These dreams are of enormous importance and provide a release mechanism for many people from the cares of everyday life. Under heavy sedation, as with a dose of sleeping pills, we do not dream and a vital protective mechanism of the mind is lost. Normally, we go from a light sleep to a deep sleep; when we awaken, we can turn over and go to sleep again. An unfamiliar sound will wake us up at once, for our subconscious mind is always alert. When we finally wake up, we should feel completely refreshed. This is normal sleep and the type we should aim for.

The terrible, exhausting problem of insomnia can be helped with self-hypnosis. We can learn a way of putting ourselves to sleep and the sleep is a normal sleep. If there are times when we do not succeed, nothing is lost. The first thing to do is to make sure you are tired and that there is nothing on your mind to keep you awake. If there is, try writing it down on a pad beside the bed (add to it during the night if necessary) — tomorrow is another day. Remember that problems are meant to be worked out during the day; at night, the mind is to be refreshed. It is also vitally important that the bed is comfortable, after all we spend a third of our lives there, and that you, too, are comfortable — not too hot or cold, and with an empty bladder. These are the physical requirements of sleep. Now for the mental ones.

If we lie in bed feeling happy that we are resting and thinking pleasant thoughts, putting all our unresolved problems out of our minds as far as possible, then we can start to use certain techniques to induce sleep. We can relax one part of the body after another, starting with the feet and moving upwards. We can count slowly and with each count drift deeper and deeper asleep. On occasions when I have had trouble sleeping, I would put myself to sleep by saying one thing as I breathed in and another as I breathed out. Everyone will have their own words, but the ones I used which worked perfectly were, 'I will go to sleep' as I inhaled and 'I must go to sleep' as I exhaled. My sleeping pattern returned and I was able to get to sleep within ten breaths after I had absorbed the idea. This may take a couple of weeks to master, but it is well worth the persistent effort. If distracting thoughts disturb you, or if you wake up, you must start again and establish that peaceful rhythm which, in most cases, will induce sleep.

This method has been used many, many times by patients and while it does not work for everybody, at least it helps some to find a way of sleeping better. Even if you cannot sleep, but lie awake resting with your mind at peace, you are reviving yourself and may find, in some ways, it is partly as good as sleep itself. By trying too hard to sleep, you will most likely be kept awake.

Using sleeping tablets as an aid can, of course, provide relief. But their use is limited and once started the habit is difficult to stop except with great determination. Deep relaxation is a far better method to develop and one which can be used as you reduce the nightly dose. Remember, too, that certain brands are more addictive than others, so ask your doctor's advice.

12: Warts

The fact that warts disappear with hypnotherapy is a challenge in itself, because how can we be sure that their disappearance is due to the treatment given. Actually, I believe we can because when we take warts that have been present for many years and which disappear in a couple of weeks, and when we then multiply the large number of cases in which this is almost invariably the result, then we can be sure. I have treated some people who did not get better, but the vast majority did. I shall cite a few cases.

A little boy, aged about 12, came to me with 76 warts on his body. He had had these for many years. Under hypnosis, I removed about half of them painlessly and then decided to leave him with the suggestion that the ones I had not touched would fall off of their own accord. When I saw him next, about two weeks later, he was entirely free of warts and a much happier young lad.

A nun came to see me, suffering from verrucae on her feet. She had been to various specialists, both in Ireland and England, and had been treated over a number of years to no effect. I hypnotised her, but as she was leaving she told my secretary that she thought the treatment was quite useless. However, she returned three months later to tell me that her verrucae had dropped off completely and she was cured at last.

A man I treated in a military hospital had a large number of warts on his hands. Once again, he had had these for years. I hypnotised him and told him to come back the following week. When I saw him next, his warts had not dropped off, but they had turned black. This was an intriguing case for me and something completely different to the usual reaction, where the warts died and the skin returned to normal. In this case, the man's warts were half-dead. I called in the other doctors in the hospital to see this unusual case, but this had the wrong effect on the patient: with all the attention, he felt a certain incredulity about the effectiveness of hypnosis and the following week when he came back, the warts had started to grow again. So I hypnotised him once more and with further suggestion, the warts dropped off.

PART IV: MISCELLANEA

1: Last Days at the Hospital

Fifty-five years ago, I stood in the entrance hall of the Royal College of Surgeons in Dublin, along with all the other candidates for the Fellowship. We were waiting to hear our fate. One by one, as our names were called, we walked slowly up the staircase, which seemed longer and wider than usual. I knew that I had been cheeky entering this examination; I had put in a late application, since we had to state that we were over 25 and I was under this age on the closing date. I hoped that my inexperience would be compensated for by my enthusiasm and love of surgery. I had visited all the hospitals in Dublin so frequently that I knew almost every patient who was presented in the clinical examination. I also knew the whims of almost all the examiners, so I had to keep my tongue firmly in my cheek as I answered the questions with what I hoped was an air of authority.

The failure rate for these types of examination was, and is, very high. I was to be told any moment now whether I was to be one of the majority of candidates who would walk back down the stairs with a crest-fallen face, or one of the minority allowed to descend wearing the gown of a Fellow of the College. My lack of experience (only three months post-graduate surgery) nearly brought me down, but my enthusiasm won the day — I was wearing the robes of a Fellow when I walked down the stairs. Although humble in my inexperience and still wondering at my nerve, I felt elated — I was the youngest Fellow of the College to date. At the bottom of the staircase I was met by the Registrar whose words of encouragement I shall never forget. (The reader should not feel that any qualified surgeon in 1989 is so inexperienced! Nowadays, no one is elected a Fellow of the Royal College of Surgeons without having had years of post-graduate work.)

I have had a long innings and in many ways I feel as fit as I did half a century ago, when I made that essential first step into a surgical career — a day which brought me an almost unreal sense of joy, saddened somewhat by the despondent faces of those who walked away without a gown. I felt like the final transition from tadpole into frog. Since then, I have had many thrilling and exciting times. My work has been extremely rewarding and fulfilling.

What is most needed in the world today is a decrease in tension and an increase in harmony, not only among people but within individuals. It is towards this end that I direct the present work, believing, as I do, in the treatment of the whole personality. If a person comes to a doctor with a duodenal ulcer caused by worry and that ulcer is operated upon without treating its cause within the patient, then the principles of the Hippocratic Oath, to which every medical practitioner is bound, are not being fulfilled. I feel that there is an enormous opportunity in surgical wards everywhere to promote the general health of the patient and, in fact, the health of the whole community.

Every case of a duodenal ulcer, or any of the other myriad complaints described in these pages, should be examined for its cause, which is usually stress of some kind. As a rule, it should be identified and treated first. I would like every patient suffering with a duodenal ulcer to be given a cassette on the use of relaxation in overcoming anxiety, as a matter of course.

I am a firm believer in the treatment of the whole person, not just the diseased part. Any member of the medical profession is welcome to see the case sheets of those patients I mention in this book, although the stories have been written in such a way as to protect the identity of my patients, except where permission has been granted. A few of the case histories are included simply to show the power of the mind over the body, showing, on the one hand, the enormous potential reserves which the human race possesses and, on the other, how our own mind control, rather than drugs, can be harnessed to our great advantage.

I will devote the last few pages of this book to some of the cases I dealt with during my last working week in hospital, in the summer of 1979.

A girl of nineteen was sent to me as a potential case for a gastrectomy operation, or the removal of part of the stomach. She had had 'full medical treatment', that is, she had been in hospital for six weeks under medical supervision and had not responded. I asked her if anyone had inquired whether she had some worry on her mind, to which she said, 'No'. I then asked her if there was. 'Yes', she replied and proceeded to tell me the problem. Not unpredictably perhaps, her worry concerned a young man. The answer to me was obvious. She accepted my suggestion and, under hypnosis, her pain rapidly disappeared. There was no need for a gastrectomy.

On Monday morning, before my surgical out-patients' session was due to start, I had four car-accident patients to deal with. One was a young man in great pain from a broken leg. Both bones were fractured and his leg was in one of the new type of splints, an inflatable bag that steadies the leg and diminishes the bleeding, but does not stop all pain. An X-ray had already been taken and, while I was examining the other patients, he was put into bed, where I saw him. Any movement caused him intense pain and the foot was rotated outward in a very bad position. I showed him how to relax, asking him, as far as it was within his power, to think of his leg as not belonging to him, of it becoming less painful and, if he felt any suggestion of pain, to allow himself to relax deeper still — and to tell me about it. When I pulled on his leg, he had the sensation of the pain lessening and did not even feel the bones being put back into position. With someone holding his foot, we then put on a plaster cast while he was still in bed. Further X-rays revealed the bones to be in a good position.

On Wednesday, the week got into full swing. A woman of 84 was brought into our casualty department with a fractured and badly displaced wrist. The most common procedure with this type of 'Colles' fracture in most hospitals is to give a general anaesthetic, after waiting for the stomach to empty, and then to reduce the swelling. The results are usually excellent: the patient is generally discharged within a day, although an elderly one, such as this lady, would be kept in for a little longer. With the present cost of hospitalisation, this treatment would run into three figures.

At 84 years of age, however, an anaesthetic is not entirely without risk. With hypnosis, there is no danger whatever. The procedure that morning was routine for me. The lady was seated and told that her wrist would be made more comfortable. Her hand was gently taken and a light pull exerted on it, with the suggestion that as the arm became straighter, she would feel more comfortable. I also suggested that she allow all the muscles in her body to relax, while still sitting firmly on the chair. A very slight pull was exerted and, as the patient felt a corresponding relief from pain, this was increased. She showed some signs of discomfort, so the pull was diminished with the suggestion that she relax more deeply, one limb after the other. (Frequently, with people who are in total rapport, a suggestion can be given that their eyes will become heavy and, with this, they may drift away into oblivion. This is not the normal procedure, however, as freedom from pain is, as a rule, rapidly obtained.) I took the woman's hand and pulled hard. Finally, with an assistant holding her arm, I exerted great force, very steadily and almost painlessly. The wrist could now be bent forward with ease. The bones felt in good position and I applied a plaster cast. A check X-ray was taken which showed the bones satisfactorily in position. I gave her instructions about what to do if her hand were to swell and on how to move her fingers. She felt very happy to be freed so quickly from her pain and when her check X-ray had been examined, she was allowed home, expressing her gratitude as do all who have had a Colles fracture immediately and painlessly reduced on attending hospital.

On our operating list that morning, there was a case marked down as a 'carbuncle in a diabetic'. I saw the patient then for the first time. His diabetes was not under complete control and he had a discharging abscess, which had a number of openings and looked to the recently qualified doctors like a carbuncle. It was, in fact, an old cyst, which had become septic and burst through different openings. Keeping a diabetic without food and giving a general anaesthetic is not desirable, indeed it can be dangerous. If the patient had been a good hypnotic subject, the problem would, of course, have been non-existent. But he was not and so I used a compromise. I told the nurses that they should give him a meal, since he was not going to have a general anaesthetic. Thus, the treatment of his diabetes was not interrupted. Then, in the ward, I showed him how to relax and, on the operating table, he relaxed sufficiently to allow me to make a three-quarter incision over the abscess without him even feeling the sensation of being touched. When the lining of the cyst was being removed, however, he did feel some pain, so it was gently curetted, or scraped, instead and then the wound packed. This caused him some slight discomfort, but he shrugged it off as virtually nothing. He was delighted at having had the job done without the treatment of his diabetes being interrupted and with the minimum of pain. He was allowed to go home immediately afterwards.

The same objects had been achieved as in the case of the

elderly lady with the fractured wrist: the saving of discomfort to the patient, as well as the saving of urgently needed bed-space, staff time and tax-payers' money. True, it took an extra few minutes of the surgeon's valuable time, but it saved that of the anaesthetist.

Two telephone calls came through which, to say the least, I found interesting. One was from a man who wanted help with his shyness, something which had started as fear resulting from his brother's death in a car crash. They used to share a room and when, as a little boy he went to bed at night, he was filled with a terror that gradually increased until any creaking of boards in the house would frighten him. This terror lessened as he got older, but he developed such a fear of meeting people that he hated to leave the house and would only do so to go to work. He rang me because, ten years previously, he had played the record *How to Stop Smoking* and had never smoked since; he thought that possibly the same techniques could release him from his intense fear and shyness.

Then I received a telephone call from a woman whose elderly father was in hospital in Dublin and would have to have a gangrenous foot removed. But he was refusing a general anaesthetic, declaring he would only have it removed under hypnosis. His daughter asked if I could take him into our hospital. He had undergone an hernia operation here many years ago with hypnosis and a local anaesthetic. She added that unless we complied with his request, he was going to die. Her call was followed by a letter from the hospital, asking if we could admit the man and stating that he wished to be 'near his own people'. Since he came from the area our hospital serves, it was actually the correct place for him to be.

He arrived on Thursday. He had a very bad chest and it was for this reason that, ten years ago, I had used hypnosis on him. At that time, he smoked a hundred cigarettes a day and even though he had cut down considerably, the damage to his blood vessels was such that when a heavy weight fell on his foot, it had turned gangrenous. The circulation in his other foot was poor and my house surgeon informed me it would have to be amputated, too, in time. He added that the patient's mind was somewhat disorientated, although I think this was perhaps due to the pain-killing drugs he had been given. I asked the old man how the accident had happened and I am sure that, had he not been so humorous in his description, I would have found if difficult to follow his rambling explanation. He explained that someone had shown him a very heavy object, asking him how much he thought it had cost, to which he replied that it was no use asking the value of an article like that: 'Had he asked me the cost of the tail-board of an ass' cart, I could have told him ' — his expression was so amusing, I actually made a note of it at the time. This was in fact the object that had later slipped and fallen on his foot, crushing it.

I showed him how to relax and the pain in his leg rapidly diminished. The smell from the gangrenous foot was horrible and there was nothing to be gained by waiting any longer to operate. I put him down second on the list for Friday and performed the operation myself, amputating his foot under local anaesthetic and hypnosis. He suffered no pain or shock. A couple of days later, his other leg showed signs of improvement since his system was no longer absorbing poisons from the gangrenous foot.

This was my last case for that day. The next day I retired from the hospital. I called in to see the old man at a later date and found him well. I was glad that the amputation had been successful. It was the last operation I was to perform.

2: How to Relax and use Self-Hypnosis

The whole world needs to relax and almost everybody feels the need. It is one thing to be told to relax and another thing to be able to do so. My aim is to teach you the principles of relaxation and to show you how you can relax as deeply as a person who allows himself to be operated on under hypnosis. Not all of us can relax to this extent, but we all can put right those thoughts in our subconscious minds that make us react in a way that causes us harm or displeasure. It is, of course, essential beforehand to have reasoned out, with the conscious mind, as honestly as possible, the cause of our problems. Then, and only then, should we try to reach into our subconscious minds and emotions, the crucial factor being that there must be harmony between our feelings in the subconscious and our reasoning in the conscious. It is essential that these emotions are right, for they govern to a large extent our actions.

The principles of reaching into our emotions to overcome pain is something we can do relatively easy if the pain is brought on by dwelling on it. It may be a very severe pain and yet the cause of it is often quite simple. We can get rid of this pain, either completely or almost completely, by relaxing. (Almost completely is in many ways better because we can keep training ourselves to get rid of the little bit that remains.) If the pain comes from cancer, it may be that there is a psychological element involved, for the pain may be felt intensely and yet the original cause may not be so great. We can overcome the intense pain, but the original pain must be dealt with at a much deeper level.

So, firstly, we must set out to do as much honest thinking and adjusting as we are consciously, and conscientiously, capable of doing. After that, we can use the principles of relaxation and self-hypnosis to reach the deepest crevices of our minds and the deepest recesses of our emotions, in order to allow the truths which we accept in our conscious reason to infiltrate completely into our whole being, to find the harmony which alone brings freedom. It is this harmony that leads to achievement and success, for it will be generally admitted that when our emotions are in conflict with our will, then our emotions almost invariably prevail.

Using self-hypnosis to overcome the spasm of an asthma attack is usually very simple and successful because, logically, we know that the spasm is doing us harm. Most of us who are suffering from asthma have already been given various medications to paralyse the muscles that go into spasm; we are, therefore, in no doubt that they are better out of spasm. Self-hypnosis for asthma, however, can only be used to correct symptoms; if we are to effect a complete cure, we must search for the cause, just as we must with other forms of stress. We must be prepared to make all sorts of logical adjustments.

It is important to be sincere about this exercise. With sincerity of intention, reaching into the emotions becomes proportionately easier; if you are only partially keen on achieving harmony, then you are likely to achieve it only partially. An example of this is someone who, knowing that smoking is likely to cause a great deal of suffering, still retains reservations about quitting. In such a case, it is not nearly so easy to reach into one's emotions and achieve harmony. But, if one has honestly decided never to take nicotine again, then one is able to transfer this thought into the subconscious.

The same, of course, applies to someone who is deriving some advantage from an illness. Very often, the 'ill' person gains sympathy and a great deal of attention, having many things done for them because of the illness. If this applies to us, even in a small measure, it is essential that we view being well as being of much greater benefit to us than the relatively small gains we may make from being sick.

When consciously, therefore, we realise that the disadvantages of a given condition far outweigh the advantages, the result is a heightened desire to get rid of the condition. Reaching the emotions then becomes proportionately easier, compared to a state of partial desire in which we wish to hold on to the symptoms that bring the benefits. In other words, before we can hope to achieve the freedom that comes from reaching into our subconscious, we should make absolutely sure that the whole of our reasoning is in agreement about achieving it.

If we have problems on our minds, problems that are difficult to put aside for even a short time, then it is wise to write them down and place the piece of paper beside us when we are relaxing. In this way, we realise that the problems are not likely to be forgotten and can be dealt with later. With that made clear, we can proceed with the practice.

With deep relaxation, a part of the mind is awake, while a part of it goes to sleep. This may not be absolutely accurate, but it is the easiest way to understand what happens. You do not go fully to sleep. Your eyes may feel very heavy and stuck together and you may feel a delightful sense of peace. This need not frighten you because with the slightest desire to waken up you can do so. Or if you want to be more definite you can say to yourself, 'wake up': your eyes are no longer sticky and you have a feeling of real calm and relaxation. One patient described the sensation to me. She was a diver and her image was of water: she said it was like sinking downwards, slowly and weightlessly, floating in absolute peace, and the waking up, like rising, in slow but deliberate motion, to a calm, flat surface.

Here is one of the ways of relaxing. I have used it about 50,000 times. It was reckoned that I used it some 40,000 times in hospital, including several thousand operations in surgery with no form of anaesthetic except hypnosis.

Find a comfortable position, sitting in an armchair or on a couch. Make sure you are not likely to be disturbed. If you have things on your mind that might disturb you when you are relaxing, write them down and put them beside you.

Try and let all your body relax, sit back and look up at the ceiling. If your eyes feel a little more comfortable closed, then allow them to shut, for you can concentrate better with no distractions. Let every muscle in your body relax as far as you can. Start with the right arm, the right shoulder, the biceps, the right elbow, the forearm, the right wrist and the fingers. Let the left arm relax the same way — the shoulder, the biceps, the elbow, the forearm, the wrist and the fingers. Let the left leg relax. Let the right leg relax. The left thigh relax. The right thigh relax, the left knee, the right knee. Let the left calf relax, the right calf relax, the left ankle, the right ankle. Let both feet relax. Let your abdomen relax. Let your chest relax. Let your neck relax, let the face relax. Allow the jaw to relax. Allow the muscles in the cheeks to relax. Allow the muscles that move the eyes and the muscles that move the forehead to relax. In fact, let every muscle in your body relax, including the muscles behind the head and neck, behind and between the shoulders and down the back.

Allow the mind to relax, just as the body. As you think of relaxing, you relax more and more. Listen to your breathing and count in your mind as you breathe in and out: 1, 2, relax deeper and deeper and deeper, 3, 4, 5, deeper still and deeper still and deeper still, 6, 7 — by now your eyes should feel like shutting, if they haven't already. If they are open, allow them to shut now; 8, 9, 10, deeper and deeper still. It may be that now you are feeling very relaxed. Or it may be that you are still feeling you cannot do so. But in this relaxed position, you are more likely to accept the thoughts in the deeper parts of your mind. You can easily go over the parts of the body again, speaking quietly and with sincerity.

Now allow yourself to relax deeper and deeper and deeper still. You are going on a holiday, all your expenses have been paid and you are going to a part of the world where you would be immeasurably happy. You can picture yourself going off to play golf or to swim in the sea, or lying on the beach or walking along a beautiful lane that leads to a garden of such magnificence that you feel in a dream-like state when walking through it. Now relax more and more and more, and think of this garden with the path and in it, beautiful plants and trees and shrubs. The garden is some distance from you, but as you walk down the lane each step you take brings you further along and nearer to it and you feel more relaxed and more relaxed as you walk down the lane. Then you come to a sudden turn and you are surprised by all the beauty before you, because you are coming straight into the garden. The sun is shining, the white clouds are floating overhead in the blue sky. The green trees match the green grass and around it all, the flowers are growing and the scent is intoxicating. And overhead you can hear the birds singing in the trees and you feel life is wonderful. As you walk around and around the garden in peace, you find things growing in such abundance and with such a flourish that you wonder how the ground can be so rich and all the plants flowering at the same time. You wish you could take some of them home with you.

As you are wishing this, a friend sees you in the garden and she comes along and tells you how she, too, has found this place where everybody is so happy and so relaxed, and you decide to sit down with her and talk. But a man walks up to you and his face is so relaxed and he is so happy that you are drawn to him. And now you have the choice of either a man or a woman to speak to. You look around for two chairs and sit down. You want to know what brought him to this magnificent garden of peace and he tells you the story of all the things he has done and what happened to him. He relates absolutely to yourself and you feel you have found a real friend. You tell him about yourself and your problems seem to dissolve as you see the answer. So you go on through all the problems in your life, knowing that there is something you can do or think that can bring you at least part of the serenity that your friend has, as you and he talk on and on until the time comes that you decide to go home. And as you walk up the lane, you find that there is more beauty than you knew when you were coming down. You see the birds building their nests, the flowers starting to bud. Now, as you reach home, you know that you have relaxed deeply and that you will continue to relax each day.

By this time, with all the body feeling comfortable and the mind more at peace, some will have found themselves in a very receptive frame of mind. It does no harm, however, to go on relaxing more and more, but this time, counting. Now, count slowly, perhaps up to ten. Then turn your attention to the problem that is on your mind — the relief of pain, itchiness of the skin, some great annoyance, spasm from asthma, a headache. Keep in mind what you believe to be true — that the pain, or whatever it is, is serving no useful purpose, that you have made certain from your doctor that there is no further special treatment required. You can then think along the line that the deeper mind has the function of cutting off unimportant sensations. You should find as you think of this that the pain sensations will lessen and perhaps disappear. In fact, the spasm of asthma may go incredibly quickly; an ordinary headache can similarly disappear, even as a severe migraine, in time, can go.

Naturally, various problems have to be tackled differently. If you are using self-hypnosis for the relief of discomfort you may find, on counting, say, up to five, that the pain is a little better. You can then count on and find the pain gradually lessen until you reach the stage where there is so little left that you are no longer concerned about it.

If you are taking away a tension headache, it is quite useful to carry on relaxing deeper and deeper with each breath until you can feel a delightful sensation of relief. Moving your head about, you can find it free of pain and tension in the muscles of the neck. With an itch or spasm of asthma, you can wake yourself when you feel relief. With insomnia, however, you can stay in this relaxed state and simply drift into sleep.

Before waking yourself, you can think along the lines of developing a reflex action whereby any potentially stressful situation can instantaneously trigger off the feeling of being calm, collected and at your best — in full possession of your faculties. If you are using self-hypnosis to free yourself from withdrawal symptoms (perhaps hard drugs or nicotine), you can visualise yourself in a peaceful scene, maybe lying in the sun, listening to the lapping of the waves — totally relaxed, the sun seeping into your body, and you feel completely free from any desire to take anything which might spoil this feeling.

When you have made the decision, in a relaxed frame of mind as well as in your conscious reasoning, that you are going to face every problem squarely as it arises, then you can expect a cure. When you relax naturally, you can feel at times that nothing is happening, yet, on thinking of your particular problem, you may find that it has gone.

It is difficult, sometimes, to follow instructions or suggestions given in writing. It is particularly difficult when trying to learn self-hypnosis, since the brain has to work hard at a time when we wish it to be as relaxed as possible. For this reason, cassettes can make practice immeasurably easier. With one of these, you can sit and relax, listening effortlessly to a suggestion. And then, having learned how to reach into your emotions, you can work entirely on your own, keeping the cassette in some handy place where it can be used again when required.

On 11 May 1982, a lecture was given at the Royal Society of Medicine in London, on terminal care. This is a difficult subject and one we do not like to face, but the fact is that we all have to die sometime and we may as well enjoy it if we can. The lecturer showed photographs of people who had been in agony and whose pain-relievers were not fully able to alleviate the pain. Hypnosis or self-hypnosis was used on those who knew that their condition was incurable. These photographs showed people with a smile on their faces, people in idyllic peace. This lecture on hypnosis and terminal care was undoubtedly in the highest traditions of medical practice.

MEDICAL HYPNOSIS SOCIETIES WORLDWIDE

International Society of Hypnosis
R.O. Stanley, Administrative Officer, Department of Psychiatry, University of Melbourne, Austin Hospital, Heidelberg, Victoria 3084, Australia.

CANADA: Ontario Society of Clinical Hypnosis
Mrs Lee Marks, Suite 402, 200 St Clair Avenue West, Toronto, ON M4V 1R3.

ENGLAND: British Society of Experimental and Clinical Hypnosis
Dr Michael Heap, Psychology Department, Middlewood Hospital, Sheffield S6 1TP.
British Society of Medical and Dental Hypnosis
Mrs M. Samuels, 42 Links Road, Ashstead, Surrey KT21 2HJ.

WEST GERMANY: Deutsche Gessellschaft fur Artzlichi Hypnose und Autogenes Training
Dr Ivansonn, 1st President, Brinderkrankenhauq, Saafig D–5471.

INDIA: Indian Society for Clinical and Experimental Hypnosis
Dr H. Jana, Udyan Marg, Ellis Bridge, Ahmedabad, Gujarat 380006.

IRELAND: Irish Society for Clinical and Experimental Hypnosis
Dr P.J. Browne, Psychiatric Unit, Cork Regional Hospital, Cork.

ISRAEL: Israel Society for Clinical and Experimental Hypnosis
Dr Karl Fuchs, 44 Hanassi Avenue, Haifa 34643.

ITALY: Centro Studi de Ipnosi Clinica e Psiocoterapie 'H. Bernheim'
Dr G. Guantieri, Via Valverde 65, Verona 37122.

NETHERLANDS: Nederlandse Vereniging Voor Hypnotherapie
Dr F.P. Bannick, Postbus 4085, 3502 HB Utrecht.

SCOTLAND: Scottish Branch — British Society of Medical and Dental Hypnosis
Dr M.S. Seltzer, 5 Arran Drive, Glasgow, G46 7NL.

SOUTH AFRICA: South African Society of Clinical Hypnosis
Dr J. Leeb, P.O. Box 908-550, Montana 0151, Pretoria.

SWEDEN: Swedish Society for Clinical and Experimental Hypnosis
Mr Kjell Waara, Box 269, S–61126, Nykoping.

SWITZERLAND: Swiss Medical Society of Hypnosis
Dr Med. V. Schnurigen, Bahnhofplatz 1, CH–5400, Baden.

USA: American Society of Clinical Hypnosis
Mr William Hoffman, Jr., Suite 336, 2250 East Devon Avenue, Des Plaine, IL 60018.

SELF-HYPNOSIS RELAXATION TAPES

Dr Jack Gibson devised and produced a series of self-hypnosis recordings as a post-treatment aid to patients, which were probably the first of their kind available, in the 1950s. Over the years, he has revised and re-recorded these on cassette and added to the range of psychosomatic disorders covered. Generally, the tapes discuss the nature of the particular problem on Side 1 and then explain how to practise deep relaxation in relation to that problem on Side 2. The tapes may not always effect a cure, but when used properly they will, in almost all cases, be a help. They can be used as a 'booster' if and when required. Cassettes in the series include:

ACCIDENTS: *How to recover from an accident* (MD7)
Dr Crowe, the American orthopaedic surgeon who coined the phrase 'whiplash injury', has said, 'This record should be used by everybody involved in an accident'.

ACNE: *How to be free from acne* (MD14)
Acne appears to be connected with the stress involved in making the transition from childhood to adulthood. Relaxation can have an enormously beneficial effect on the condition of the skin.

ACTORS: *Relaxation for actors* (MD21)
It is often said that tension is good for an actor. Not so— a relaxed actor, who retains all the alertness and keenness necessary, is at his or her best.

ADOLESCENCE: *Before the age of involvement* (MD31)
This is the only tape in the series which does not use self-hypnosis. It discusses sex education frankly and in such a way that parents and children can listen to it together in an atmosphere of ease and freedom.

ANOREXIA: *How to be free from anorexia* (MD10)
This explains how people who suffer from extreme thinness can get to love their natural appearance. In fact, it is worthwhile for anyone who has a tendency to be very thin to listen to it. It does not, however, deal with the medical complications of anorexia and so people should also attend their doctor.

ARTHRITIS: *Relief from arthritis* (MD13)
Nothing can be done to cure this condition, but much can be done to give relief from pain and by getting the hormones to work more perfectly, general health can be improved. A life of misery can be turned into a life of happiness.

ASTHMA: *Relief from asthma* (MD23)
All forms of asthma are in a sense psychosomatic and all asthmatics, especially children, can learn how to take away their attacks. One side of the cassette is for adults and the other for children. Since most adults

suffered their first attack in childhood, it is recommended that they listen to both sides. It is also recommended that parents listen to the tape with their afflicted child. All asthmatic children can benefit from the relaxation methods advocated, even those who do not respond and who should be under a doctor's care.

BED-WETTING: *Overcoming nocturnal enuresis* (MD9)
When a tensed child, or even young adult, learns to relax, he will go to sleep with less on his mind. The bladder will fill normally and when it is full, the sensation will awaken him. Some children who listen to this tape can be dry from the first night; with others, it takes longer for the natural reflex to be regained. It is desirable that parents listen to the tape with their children at least once.

BINGE-EATING: *How to stop binge-eating* (MD25)
It is essential to stop eating when we have had enough. Learning how to do this, or getting the motivation to do it, is the subject of this tape.

BLUSHING: *How to stop blushing* (MD20)
By forgetting about ourselves, we can stop blushing. This tape explains how we can get over this self-consciousness; in fact, there is no other way of overcoming the condition.

BUSINESS: *Efficiency in business* (MD24)
By really learning how to relax, we can make our lives better and our businesses more prosperous.

CHILDBIRTH: *Towards painless childbirth* (MD2)
If relaxation is practised from the beginning of pregnancy, it is possible to control morning sickness, learn to remain undisturbed by the baby's movements and cope with the attendant problems of being pregnant. By the time the baby is due to be born, practice in deep relaxation can make the experience of giving birth a relatively painless and pleasurable one.

DERMATITIS: *Relief from dermatitis* (MD28)
Many forms of dermatitis, especially psoriasis, respond well to relaxation treatment. Once the itching sensation is removed, the rash itself can disappear in a remarkably short time.

DRINKING: *How to stop drinking* (MD6)
This tape is intended for people who are drinking heavily and wish to stop. It is enjoyable.

DRINKING: *How to reduce your drinking* (MD43)
We can get just as much pleasure out of three pints as we can out of six. This tape shows you how.

FEAR: *How to conquer fear* (MD12)
This tape is aimed at showing people how to deal with irrational fears, especially agoraphobia.

FLYING: *Flying without fear* (MD18)
There are thousands of people who are terrified by the thought of flying; there are as many more who feel they would be unhappy in an airplane. This tape helps them to be free.

MIGRAINE: *Relief from migraine* (MD26)
With this painful condition, tension causes the nervous system to relay messages to the blood vessels which go into spasm and then dilate, causing extreme pain. This can be relieved by relaxing and reaching into the subconscious mind to correct the confused thoughts that cause the tension. Positive messages sent to the blood vessels maintain their normal level of tone.

NAIL-BITING: *How to stop nail-biting* (MD8)
Many people's nails are bitten to the end. They can have the joy of seeing them grow again.

PAIN: *Relief from pain* (MD29)
When our subconscious mind understands that a pain is serving no useful purpose, it is able to cut it off. Tension intensifies pain; relaxation relieves it; deep relaxation can eliminate it. It is possible to remove the pain sensation so completely that a surgeon can operate without the use of an anaesthetic. If only a portion of such relief is attained, it is worthwhile.

PERIOD PAIN: *Relief from dysmenorrhoea* (MD35)
Dysmenorrhoea is one of the many painful conditions that responds to hypnotherapy. We can learn through relaxation how to achieve the correct balance of hormones during the monthly cycle.

PREMENSTRAL TENSION: *How to be free from premenstral tension* (MD22)
With relaxation, the hormones are produced in the correct quantity. When we are relaxed, an unexpected freedom from tension can result.

RELAXATION AND PERFECTIONISM: *The art of relaxation* (MD30)
This is perhaps the most popular cassette. The ability to relax is within anyone's reach and it is one of the most important things to learn in life. Side 1 explains how by facing up to our worries, we can achieve private release and public achievement. Perfectionism can be the cause of many problems. Most people do not think of themselves as perfectionists, but this condition can manifest itself in many ways, discussed on Side 2.

SLEEP: *How to sleep better* (MD5)
Millions suffer from an inability to sleep properly. Many resort to sleeping tablets or alcohol. This cassette aims to help sufferers of insomnia regain a natural sleep pattern. Unlike sleeping tablets, the technique of deep relaxation gains in response and effectiveness with use. It helps eliminate the subconscious origins of insomnia and achieve a degree of mental harmony not previously experienced. This is the most important prerequisite for sleep.

SMOKING: *How to enjoy stopping smoking* (MD41)
It is possible to stop smoking and not to experience severe withdrawal symptoms. But the decision to stop must come from within yourself. This tape helps reinforce your decision. Thousands of people who have listened to this tape have become free, and remained free, from the addiction of nicotine.

SNORING: *How to be undisturbed by snoring* (MD34)
The subconscious mind cuts out unimportant sounds. If we can get the idea into our minds that the person snoring beside us is our real friend, we can actually learn to use the snoring sound to put ourselves to sleep.

STAMMERING: *How to be free from stammering* (MD11)
Self-consciousness very often leads to stammering. If we can learn not to think of ourselves as so important, but rather concentrate on what we have to say as being important, then the stammer can disappear. Stammering can also be caused by a fear buried in the subconscious; deep relaxation can help reveal this fear to you and remove the cause of the problem.

STUDY: *How to study and pass exams* (MD15)
We all have the ability to learn and retain information. By allowing certain principles to sink into the subconscious, we can learn and remember. 'Exam nerves' can also be controlled by relaxation.

WARTS: *How to rid yourself of warts* (MD42)
Most people have heard of warts being cured by peculiar methods. They all have an element of suggestion. Hypnosis appears to have a success rate which far outstrips other methods. It may be due to immune bodies, fibrous tissues or the blood supply being cut off, or possibly all three.

WEIGHT: *How to enjoy losing weight* (MD36)
Many of the feelings which lead to overeating are embedded in our subconscious mind since childhood — 'don't waste, eat up, finish what's on your plate'. Mind control, through self-hypnosis, is immensely more pleasant than diets or drugs. This cassette aims to bring back our natural love for food and to reinforce our instinctive hatred for excess, allowing us to attain, and maintain, our proper body weight.

These cassettes are available directly from MediDisc Limited, St David's Castle, Naas, Co. Kildare, Ireland. Telephone: (045) 97389. Price £7.95 (includes p&p).

NOTE: IT IS INADVISABLE TO PLAY THESE CASSETTES WHILE DRIVING OR ENGAGED IN DANGEROUS WORK.